THE FICTION FIX

The Fiction Fix

Stories that Heal, Empower & Transform Us

Louisa Nedkov

Shamrock Heart Press
Toronto, Ontario

"A reader lives a thousand lives before he dies. The man who never reads lives only one."

– George R.R. Martin

THE FICTION FIX
Stories that Heal, Empower & Transform Us

© 2025 Louisa Nedkov. All rights reserved.
Originally registered with the subtitle *How Stories Heal, Empower & Transform Us*.

No part of this publication may be reproduced, stored in a retrieval system, or transmitted in any form or by any means—electronic, mechanical, photocopying, recording, or otherwise—without prior written permission from the author, except in the case of brief quotations embodied in critical articles or reviews.

Disclaimer This book is offered for inspiration only and is not a substitute for professional medical or psychological advice. Please consult a qualified professional for any concerns related to your well-being.

First edition
ISBN 978-0-9684413-3-6 (hardcover)
ISBN 978-0-9684413-2-9 (softcover)
ISBN 978-0-9684413-4-3 (e-book)
Library and Archives Canada Cataloguing in Publication
CIP Data available upon request

Published by Shamrock Heart Press
Ontario, Canada

Cover design, typesetting & interior illustrations by
Barış Şehri *please visit* sehribookdesign.com

Printed in Canada

For speaking inquiries, coaching, or bulk orders:
Visit www.louisanedkov.com or www.thefictionfix.ca
This book is a work of creative nonfiction. While based on lived experiences and personal truths, all names and details have been modified for privacy and poetic integrity.

On the Origin of These Poems

The poems that have been included were created specifically for this book. Each piece was developed through a private and intentional creative process, rooted in lived experience and emotional truth. These poems are original. They have not appeared elsewhere, nor were they drawn from any shared system or public source. They were crafted and shaped to echo the voice, tone, and themes that flow through this work. They are grounded in healing, clarity, and sacred storytelling.

The author retains full rights to all poetry. Any resemblance to other works is purely coincidental. These poems belong to the soul of this book and to the quiet revolution it honours.

A Note on Spelling
As a Canadian author, the spelling throughout this book reflects Canadian English, which draws from both British and American traditions. You may notice a mix of familiar and less familiar spellings—honour, centre, aging. This is not inconsistency, but intentional alignment with Canadian usage. It reflects the linguistic blend that lives naturally in our national voice.

For Allen–

my partner in life and in love, and my best friend.

Thank you for standing beside me through every high and low, for supporting me while I disappeared into the world of these pages, and for making me laugh when I sometimes forgot how.

You brought snacks when I forgot to eat, patience when I forgot what day it was, and just the right joke when things got too serious.

Contents

The Invitation	15
A Note on Creation	16
Why I Wrote this Book	16

Part I: A Story Is the Doorway — 23
Chapter 1: A Journey Through Story — 27
Chapter 2: The Story You Needed Found You — 31
Chapter 3: The Permission to Read — 32

Part II: The Gateway of Belief — 37
Chapter 4: We Are Wired for Story — 39
Chapter 5: When a Character Feels Like Home — 40
Chapter 6: The Brain on Story — 43
Chapter 7: Imagination Is a Muscle — 47
Chapter 8: When Stories Are Too Powerful to Silence — 51
Chapter 9: The Mystery of a Sharper Mind — 58
Chapter 10: Bibliotherapy — 63
Chapter 11: Listening is Reading — 67

Part III: Stories as Sanctuary — 77
Chapter 12: Fiction as Refuge — 79
Chapter 13: The Quiet Medicine of Laughter — 92
Chapter 14: Why There Is Poetry Here — 97
Chapter 15: Sanctuary in the Wild: Nature as Healer — 101

Part IV: Stories that Heal Us — 107
Chapter 16: Stories that Heal Us — 110
    Section 1: Heartache & Healing — 113
    Section 2: Inner Struggles & Self-Perception — 144
    Section 3: Belonging & Disconnection — 170
    Section 4: Life Transitions & Identity Shifts — 186
    Section 5: Resilience & Renewal — 205

Part V: Stories that Expand Us — **241**
Chapter 17: Stories that Expand Us — 243
Chapter 18: Global Stories — 247
Chapter 19: Stories of the Displaced — 253
Chapter 20: Incarcerated Women — 259
Chapter 21: Seeing with New Eyes — 266

Part VI: Stories that Empower Us — **271**
Chapter 22: Stories that Empower Us — 273
Chapter 23: Reclaiming Her Story — 276
Chapter 24: Voice as Visibility — 281
Chapter 25: Leadership, Remembered — 286

Part VII: The Sacred Return — **293**
Chapter 26: The Sacred Return — 295
Chapter 27: The Compass Within — 299
Chapter 28: The Grace of Surrender — 303
Chapter 29: Fierce Compassion — 308
Chapter 30: The Voice that Returns — 313
Chapter 31: Aging as Awakening — 318
Chapter 32: The Frequency of Gratitude — 324
Chapter 33: Eucatastrophe, The Sacred Turn — 329
Chapter 34: The Return of Joy — 332

Epilogue — 335
Author's Note — 341
Acknowledgments — 347

The Invitation

Some stories arrive to change the world.

Others arrive to change us.

– Louisa Nedkov

The Invitation

What if you didn't need to earn your healing?

Y ou don't need to read this book perfectly. You don't need to agree with every sentence. You don't even need to read it all. You're allowed to begin from the middle. To skip a chapter or section that doesn't resonate with you. To rest when something feels too raw.

This book is not a challenge. It's a companion. A quiet place to lay things down you've carried for too long. You don't have to know exactly what you need or arrive with a plan. You're allowed to be tired, uncertain, tender.

You're allowed to read slowly. To weep. To laugh where you didn't expect to. To change your mind. To come back tomorrow—or next season. You don't need to become someone else in order to be seen here. You don't need to explain your sadness, justify your dreams, or soften your truth to make it more acceptable.

This book is here to *witness* you, not to fix you. To reflect what is sacred, not because it is polished—but because it is *real*.

Let this be your quiet permission to feel deeply and heal gently. To remember the parts of you you've had to set aside just to survive. And when you are ready to begin—not perfectly, but truthfully—turn the page. Your story, too, belongs here.

And if you're wondering how this book came to be—how these pages found their way into your hands—let me begin with the story behind the story.

A Note on Creation

This book did not begin as a book. It began as a whisper. A tug. A quiet sense that something wanted to be born through me—but only if I said yes.

So I did.

What followed wasn't tidy. It wasn't linear. Some days, I wrote with clarity. Other days, the words came like breath through fog—half-formed, half-heard, but undeniably alive.

The truth is: I didn't write every word from intellect. Some of it came through what I can only call grace.

There were moments when the language moved faster than I could think. Entire passages I reread and wondered, *Where did that come from?* And yet, there was no one else in the room. Just me—and whatever presence walks beside me when I open my heart and listen.

Yes, I wrote this book. I shaped its arc. I chose every theme. I carried it through months of doubt, devotion, and discovery. But I also know this: I did not write it alone. And perhaps that is the quiet miracle of creation.

We show up with our pens, our questions, our wonder...and something older, wiser, and kinder meets us halfway.

If this book speaks to you, may it sound not only like my voice. May it sound like your own truth returning. And may it feel, in the best and deepest way, like something that was waiting for you all along.

And once I said yes to the creative whisper, the next question arrived: *Why this book?* Why now? The answer revealed itself not all at once—but in story.

Why I Wrote this Book

I didn't know it when I began—but I was preparing for a birth. Not a metaphor. A real one. A creation shaped by months of intuition, labour, stillness, and surrender.

I never planned to write about the power of fiction to heal, empower, and transform. To soothe grief, reawaken joy, restore voice, or guide a woman back to herself. In fact, if you had told me years ago that I'd be writing an entire book about it, I probably would have laughed and said, "Fiction? You mean the thing I read on the beach?"

Like many people, I saw fiction as an escape—a luxury. Something to enjoy on vacation or on a lazy Sunday afternoon. A welcome distraction when life felt heavy, but certainly not a tool. Not something that could help me survive.

But life has a way of shaking up what you think you know—usually when you least expect it.

At first, when I sat down to write a book, I was searching for one simple, effective, and easy-to-implement tool that anyone could use to navigate the fear, burnout, and uncertainty of today's world. I did what I always do when I'm looking for answers: I returned to the research. I combed through studies in positive psychology, revisited spiritual texts that had carried me through the dark, and looked at the strategies I had studied and taught over the years.

Surely, I thought, *the answer was there.*

And then, something surprising happened. I started thinking about my own life. The moments that broke me. The moments that held me together. And I realized that the thing that had quietly, consistently carried me through it all wasn't what I'd expected.

It was fiction.

It had been there all along—lifting me, grounding me, giving me strength when I had none. It wasn't just an escape. It wasn't just entertainment. It was a lifeline.

I wrote this book because I've seen what fiction can do. I've found courage in characters who helped me keep going. I've found a gentler way to make sense of pain.

This book is for the woman who is tired but still reaching. For the reader who forgot she was allowed to feel. For the caregiver who longs to be held. For the skeptic, the seeker, the woman on the edge of reinvention.

This book isn't about escaping the world. It's about rediscovering your place in it—through stories that heal, challenge, and console. Reading fiction doesn't just pass the time. It changes us. It soothes the nervous system. It deepens empathy. It gives us a safe rehearsal space for life's hardest moments.

I didn't write this because I had all the answers. I wrote it because I've lived the questions. Because I know what it feels like to be lost, to be tired, to reach for something that doesn't fix everything—but helps you hold it.

This book was born from that quiet need. For comfort. For clarity. For something that meets you gently, without demanding more of you.

Not a manual. Not a program. Just a place to land. A companion for those days when the world feels like too much and your own voice feels far away.

I hope this book becomes that for you. A doorway to solace. A reminder that you're not alone. A soft but steady invitation to begin again—through stories that understand what you're going through, even when no one else seems to. Because fiction did that for me. And now, I offer it to you.

Perhaps it's no coincidence that by the time this book is born, I will also be something new—a certified bibliotherapist. A guide with words in one hand and a lamp in the other.

I've always believed in the power of story. But this journey showed me how stories don't just live in books. They live in us. They move through us. And sometimes, they ask to be written so they can help others heal too.

If you're holding this book, you are part of its arrival. You are part of the breath, the pause, the page, and the prayer. Thank you for walking with me. Thank you for reading with your whole self.

This book is not the end. It's the beginning of something I didn't know I was waiting for. It's a birth. And you are holding it now.

The Stories You Carry

The ones that made you.
The ones that saved you.
The ones still unfolding.

You carry them quietly—
threaded into your laughter,
stitched into your silences
woven through every breath you take.

The stories you carry are
older than memory,
older than reason,
older even than the
names you've been given.

Some of them taught you how to stay.
Some taught you how to leave.
Some taught you what
love could look like when
no one had the words for it yet.

You carry stories of breakage,
but also of beauty.
Of beginnings
you didn't ask for,
but still made your own.

You carry the stories of women
who stood before you,
and the ones
you are still becoming.

Not every story
you carry is finished.
Not every ending
has been written.

Some are still breathing in you.
Softly.
Boldly.
Bravely.

The stories you carry
are not burdens.
They are blueprints.
They are bridges.
They are seeds.

And the strength
you seek?
It was never lost.

It's written in the stories
you already carry.

A story is the doorway
What waits on the other side is you

Part I:
A Story Is the Doorway

A story is a doorway to another world.
And sometimes, when we walk through the right one—
we find ourselves waiting there.

The Door Is Open

You don't have to knock.
You've already been invited.
Not by me—
but by the part of you
that knows it's time
to feel again.

The door is open.
Not grand, not gilded—
just simple, and quiet,
like the page of a book
you've turned without meaning to,
and suddenly,
you're home.

No one will ask for explanations here.
No one needs your résumé of pain.
Just bring your breath,
your ache,
your hope—
and maybe the version of you
that hasn't had a place to land.

Stories wait,
not to fix you
but to meet you.
To remind you of softness.
To mirror your strength.

To hold the truth you've carried
longer than you should have had to.

Chapter 1: A Journey Through Story

This book was never meant to be read in one sitting. It was meant to be lived through, returned to, and gently discovered—like a house with many rooms, each one holding a different kind of knowing.

The structure of *The Fiction Fix* isn't just organizational—it's emotional. Each section was designed to mirror a kind of movement: from reflection to recovery, from inner stillness to outward empowerment, from quiet ache to sacred return.

You'll begin with the origin of the book—how it was born and why it matters—and the permission to read it in your own way. Then, slowly, we'll open the door to what fiction makes possible.

The Story Is the Doorway

We'll explore the power of story—not as escape but as entry. This section introduces fiction as a mirror, a threshold, and a quiet guide back to meaning.

The Gateway of Belief

This is where science and soul meet. If you've ever questioned whether reading can truly heal, here you'll find the neuroscience, emotional resonance, and lived proof that it can.

Stories as Sanctuary

A soft landing. In this section, fiction becomes rest, poetry becomes pause, and laughter becomes medicine. These are the stories that hold you while you gather strength.

Stories that Heal Us (The Fiction Prescriptions)
Here, life's challenges meet their literary companions—books that walk with you through grief, burnout, trauma, reinvention, and return.

Stories that Expand Us
These are the narratives that stretch the heart. Fiction that helps us see beyond borders, systems, and silence. Stories of the displaced, the incarcerated, the forgotten—and the deeply human.

Stories that Empower Us
This is where voice returns. Where women's stories rise. Where intuition, courage, and quiet fire take shape on the page—and in the self.

The Sacred Return
Not an ending, but a homecoming. This final section invites you back to your wholeness—with softness, sovereignty, and the reminder that your story is still unfolding.

There is no wrong way to move through this book. But if you choose to follow its rhythm, you may notice something subtle. Each section builds not just insight but inner spaciousness. Each story carries you, quietly, toward yourself.

Why I Call Them Book Friends
Throughout this book, you'll find curated reading lists—books paired with specific life experiences, emotional landscapes, and personal reckonings. I call them "Book Friends" not because they are casual suggestions but because they are companions. They are the books that stay with you, speak to your ache, and walk beside your becoming.

Like true friends, they don't rush you or tell you what to feel. They simply sit beside you with quiet wisdom and open arms. Some offer laughter. Some offer fire. Some will break your heart open—and gently help you gather the pieces.

They are not just recommendations. They are reflections. And sometimes, they arrive right when you need them most.

A Note on Repetition

You may notice that a few books appear more than once in these pages. This is intentional. Some stories are layered—they speak to more than one kind of ache, more than one season of the soul. A novel that offers solace in grief may also illuminate the path of self-forgiveness. Rather than confining these works to a single category, I've allowed them to appear where they're most needed.

A Note on Nonfiction

Though this book celebrates fiction, you'll find a few nonfiction titles among its pages. Their inclusion is purposeful. These books aren't here to instruct—they're here to support. To offer insight for those who wish to walk a little deeper with a theme.

They sit beside the novels, not as opposites, but as companions. Where fiction opens the heart, these texts help steady it. They're not detours—but stepping stones for those who want to keep walking.

Behind the Curation

The books shared in these pages have been selected with deep care and intention. Some I have read cover to cover—more than once. Others I've explored through excerpts, trusted reader recommendations, literary reviews, or therapeutic frameworks. In each case, I've sought to understand not just the plot, but the emotional doorway the story opens.

The "Why It Helps" reflections are not clinical prescriptions—they're intuitive invitations. They are rooted in personal resonance, reader testimony, and the quiet knowing that certain stories arrive when we need them most.

My hope is to one day read them all in full—but until then, this collection is offered as a living map: curated with discernment, guided by soul, and always open to discovery.

The Story Knows

It knows the ache beneath your laughter,
the hope you buried in a drawer,
the way your breath catches
when someone says, *"Me too."*

It waits—
not to fix you,
but to walk beside you
until the sharpness softens.

It is the mirror and the lamp,
the question and the balm.
It opens a door you forgot was there
and whispers,

"This is where your story begins again."

Chapter 2: The Story You Needed Found You

Y ou didn't go looking for it.
It found you—on a shelf, on a friend's coffee table, in a library corner you didn't mean to wander into. The story opened like a door you hadn't realized you were knocking on.

And somehow, it said exactly what you couldn't say. It held what you hadn't been able to name. It softened something sharp in you—without asking you to explain why it hurt.

You didn't know you needed it. But the story did. Because stories do that. They wait quietly for us. And, when we are ready, they speak.

You didn't pick up this book by accident. Something in you— quiet, maybe weary, maybe curious—was looking for something more. More breath. More beauty. More meaning.

This book doesn't offer perfect answers. But it offers stories. And stories are how we've always known how to make sense of life.

We tell stories to remember what matters. We read them to feel less alone. And sometimes—when we're grieving, lost, or simply tired of pretending we're fine—we reach for fiction because it's the only thing soft enough to hold us.

You don't need to be a book lover. You don't need to know where to start. All you need is a moment, a willingness to turn the page, and the openness to let a story meet you where you are.

This book is about re-entering life—with tenderness, imagination, and your heart intact—not escaping it.

Inside these pages, you'll find story companions for heartbreak, hope, resilience, burnout, loss, and healing. You'll find fiction recommendations, poems, resources, and insights.

And you'll find the space to exhale—finally.

Chapter 3: The Permission to Read

"The Story You Needed Found You" reminds us that fiction doesn't arrive like a prescription. It arrives like a friend. And that kind of arrival—quiet, intuitive, deeply felt—deserves more than apology. It deserves reverence.

Which is why we begin here...

We've been taught—especially as women—to earn our rest, justify our joy, and explain our softness. Even our stillness must be productive.

Nowhere does that quiet conditioning show up more clearly than in how we treat fiction. How often have you heard a book dismissed as "just a novel"? How often have you denied yourself the pleasure of reading because there were "more important" things to do? We tell ourselves stories about story: It's indulgent. It's lazy. It doesn't count.

But here's what I've learned from both science and lived experience: *Fiction is not a detour.* It's not a reward. It's not escape. It's restoration.

The guilt so many of us feel when we pick up a novel isn't really about time. It's about permission.

Psychologists call this *permission culture*—the idea that we must seek external validation before allowing ourselves pleasure, especially non-performative pleasure. If it doesn't produce, prove, or improve something, we struggle to let ourselves have it. But *fiction doesn't ask you to prove anything.* It asks you to feel. And that's what makes it radical. Because when we read stories, we're not zoning out. We're tuning in.

Fiction enhances *empathy*—by activating the parts of the brain responsible for understanding others. It supports *emotional regulation*—by giving us a safe space to feel big feelings without shutting down. It nourishes *imagination*—which is not a child's whim but an adult survival skill.

This is where *self-compassion*—a concept Kristin Neff explores in her powerful books like *Self-Compassion: The Proven Power of Being Kind to Yourself* and *Fierce Self-Compassion*—comes into play. Self-compassion is about treating ourselves with the same kindness we would offer to a friend in distress. Neff's work highlights how we can stop the cycle of harsh self-criticism and instead nurture ourselves with understanding, acceptance, and care. Fiction is a beautiful practice of self-compassion. It allows us to sit with our feelings without judgment and without expectation, reminding us that we are worthy of rest, softness, and emotional healing.

By allowing ourselves to sit with a novel, we are offering ourselves a *radical act of self-compassion*. We are choosing softness, recognizing that, in this moment, we are worthy of rest and emotional care—just as we would offer these things to a friend in need.

This is your invitation to dismantle the guilt around pleasure, presence, and page-turning. Because when you sit with a novel, you're not opting out of life. You're stepping back into your interior world—where healing begins.

Self-care is often sold to us in the form of bath bombs, yoga mats, and expensive retreats. But some of the deepest self-care happens quietly, when we allow ourselves to feel, to remember, to imagine.

Fiction does all three. It reminds us that we're not alone in our longings. That other people have walked this terrain before us. That even a life utterly different from our own can feel strangely familiar. And that somewhere in a character's arc, we might find the courage to trace our own.

You are allowed to rest with a book. You are allowed to choose softness. You are allowed to spend your time with beauty. Let fiction hold you. Let it speak to what has no name. Let it restore the parts of you that were never meant to be measured.

A Permission Slip

You've been told to earn your rest
to justify each quiet moment,
to explain the softness that lingers in your bones.
But what if there is no need for explanation?

What if the stillness is its own kind of revolution?
What if the story you need to hear
is the one that whispers,
"Rest.
Be still.
Let the words hold you."

In the pages of a book,
you do not need to prove,
to hustle, to strive.
Here, there is only space to feel.
To remember.
To heal.

Let the characters speak the language of your soul,
the one that has been silent too long.
Let their journey spark the courage
to trace your own.

Let fiction restore what the world forgets—
Your worth
Your joy.
Your permission.

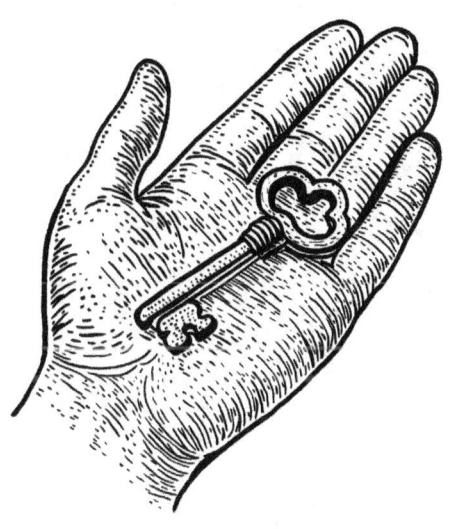

Where belief takes root, transformation begins

Part II:
The Gateway of Belief

You have felt the invitation.
Now it's time to understand the magic.

Beneath every heartbeat of story,
there is a neural spark,
a bridge between thought and feeling,
science and soul.

Welcome to the gateway of belief—
where imagination becomes transformation.

Chapter 4: We Are Wired for Story

Before there were books, there were stories.
Told around fires, carved into cave walls, painted onto clay, passed from voice to voice under starlit skies. Storytelling is older than the alphabet—older than civilization itself. It was one of the first ways in which we made sense of the world.

Anthropologists tell us that early human groups survived in part because of their ability to share information through narrative. Where danger lived. Where water could be found. Which plants could heal—and which could harm. The brain began to favour those who could listen well, remember, retell. Fiction, even then, was a rehearsal for reality.

As cultures grew, so did our stories. Myths gave shape to the mysteries of life. Epics offered moral codes and heroes to admire. Folktales taught children how to navigate their fears. In every time and place, we wrapped truth in narrative—not to deceive, but to reveal.

And we still do. We may no longer sit around the fire, but the glow of our e-readers and bedside lamps tells us the instinct lives on. We reach for fiction not only to entertain but to belong, to understand ourselves, and to feel less alone.

Because stories remind us that our lives have patterns. That pain has meaning. That joy is worth remembering. That others have suffered and survived before us—and that we can, too.

This is why fiction matters. Not just now, in this fast and fractured moment, but always. It is not a luxury. It is a lineage. Every time we read a novel, we're stepping into that long and ancient tradition of human survival, human imagination, and human connection.

We are wired for story.

And when the world feels incomprehensible, stories give us back our sense of place.

Chapter 5: When a Character Feels Like Home

Before we turn to science, let's begin with what you already know in your bones.

There's a moment many readers recognize: a line leaps off the page, a thought mirrors your own, a character feels so familiar it's almost eerie. You pause—surprised, maybe even comforted. Because somehow, that story knows something about you.

Psychologists call this *character identification*—the experience of stepping into the mind, heart, or life of a fictional person. But to readers, it feels more intimate than a definition. It's a quiet encounter with part of yourself. A remembering. A recognition. The moment isn't loud—but it lands deeply. It's like running into an old friend you've never met before.

It's not just that we understand these characters; we *feel* them. When we read emotionally rich fiction, our brain doesn't stay neutral. Our mirror neurons activate. Our limbic system lights up. The regions responsible for empathy, memory, and emotion begin to stir. We don't just observe the story—we *live* it. The boundary between "them" and "us" begins to soften.

And sometimes, what we see in a character is something we hadn't yet named in ourselves: a hidden longing, a dormant strength, or perhaps a sorrow we've been carrying without language. Their words give shape to what we haven't voiced. Their courage gives us quiet permission. Their truth becomes a lantern in our own fog.

Characters become containers for emotion—safe places to store our questions and hopes. They offer mirrors, but also maps. They don't just reflect who we are; they hint at who we might become.

They also give us rehearsal. Emotional rehearsal. Through fiction, we experience heartbreak and healing, betrayal and belonging—without the cost of consequence. We build emotional fluency. We practice forgiveness. We remember how to hope.

And as we return to them—again and again—we're often returning to parts of ourselves we'd forgotten. A younger self that still aches, an older self that knows better, a deeper self that longs to be named.

Fiction reminds us that we are not alone in our complexity. That someone else—through ink and imagination—has walked a similar emotional path. And when the world feels too loud or confusing or indifferent, these characters become companions. Quiet but unwavering, they offer presence when we most need it and language when we've lost our own.

This is why fiction matters. Not because it gives us the answers, but because it reminds us we're not the only ones asking the questions. It turns our solitude into solidarity, our searching into connection.

Because in the end, we don't just *read* great stories. We find pieces of ourselves inside them. And in finding *them*—these fictional souls carved from truth—we begin to come home.

The Ones Who Look Like Us

We meet them on the page—
a girl with a storm in her chest,
a boy afraid of being seen,
a woman who smiles while quietly unraveling.
And somehow, we know them.

We say: *That's me.*
That's what I would have said.
That's the ache I've never named.

It doesn't matter
if they live in castles, or under the sea.
We recognize ourselves anyway.

Because what we're seeing
isn't just their story.
It's the shape of our own longing.
Our hidden strength.
Our quiet rage.

We find ourselves
in their choices,
their grief,
their love that costs something.
And when they break and rise again,
we wonder if maybe we can too.

Chapter 6: The Brain on Story

You don't need to be someone who "loves science" to appreciate the power of fiction—but if you're a therapist, a doctor, a life coach, or someone who needs to understand why fiction works, then welcome. This section is for you.

Truth be told, I'm not a scientist. I don't light up at the sight of a data set. But I've worked with people long enough to know that some of us need more than instinct—we need explanation. So here it is: the neuroscience behind why story matters.

Because fiction does more than soothe us—it changes us. It doesn't just pass the time. It rewires the mind, calms the nervous system, strengthens empathy, and helps us rehearse for the hardest parts of life.

Why Your Brain Loves Stories

Long before books, stories were passed down around fires and carved into cave walls. According to Dr. Paul Armstrong, author of *Stories and the Brain*, our minds evolved not just to be entertained by stories but to use them to make sense of time, emotion, and cause and effect. Stories are how we create meaning.

Neuroeconomist Dr. Paul Zak found that character-driven stories trigger oxytocin, a hormone linked to empathy and bonding. That's why you feel connected to fictional characters. Their joys and heartbreaks become your own.

And in studies of *neural coupling*, scientists like Dr. Uri Hasson discovered that a reader's brain starts to mirror the storyteller's brain. Our minds don't just follow along—we synchronize. Story creates connection.

Fiction Calms the Nervous System

Reading silently for just six minutes reduces stress by more than 60%, according to a University of Sussex study. More effective than music or tea, fiction literally relaxes your body.

It's not passive entertainment—it's a quiet recalibration.

When we follow a cohesive, emotionally rich narrative, our minds stop spinning. Our muscles loosen. We return to coherence. And our nervous system—so often caught in fight or flight—finally finds rest.

Your Brain Doesn't Know It's Fiction

When you read about a character walking through snow, your brain's motor cortex activates as if you're taking those steps. This is called *embodied simulation*.

A study from Emory University showed that even after finishing a novel, readers had increased activity in the brain areas linked to language and physical experience—for days. Fiction leaves a lasting imprint.

Emotional Rehearsal and Resilience

Reading fiction is a safe space to feel big emotions. According to research summarized in *Brain, Mind, and the Narrative Imagination* by Ashley Taggart and Christopher Comer, fiction activates the same brain networks we use to navigate real life.

We rehearse grief, fear, hope, and transformation on the page. This builds emotional intelligence and strengthens psychological resilience. One study from the University of Buffalo even found that reading stories of adversity helped participants reframe their own life challenges.

Fiction as Empathy Training

Literary fiction enhances something called *theory of mind*—your brain's ability to understand that other people have different perspectives, feelings, and beliefs.

A 2013 study published in the journal *Science* confirmed what many intuitively know: reading literary fiction—the kind that explores inner lives and emotional nuance—improves our ability to understand the thoughts and feelings of others. Unlike genre fiction or nonfiction, these character-driven stories activate the brain's mirror neurons—the same circuits we use in real life to register empathy.

Fiction trains us to be more emotionally intelligent. It makes us better at being human.

Mental Exercise that Matters

Reading strengthens attention, memory, and cognitive flexibility. It also helps us re-learn how to concentrate in a digital world that scatters our focus.

Maryanne Wolf, in *Reader, Come Home*, explains that deep reading activates networks responsible for reflection, memory, and imagination. It builds the mind's "muscle" for sustained thought.

Stories that Stay With You

Emotionally engaging stories release dopamine, a chemical that helps the brain store information. That's why fiction stays with us far longer than lectures or checklists.

We forget bullet points. But we remember *The Color Purple*, *A Man Called Ove*, or *The Midnight Library*. Story binds emotion to memory—and that makes the lesson last.

The Brain on Story

It starts with ink on a page,
or pixels on a screen.
Nothing you can hold—
and yet, everything changes.

A single sentence
fires a dozen synapses.
A paragraph lights up your brain
like a city seen from space.

Your neurons rehearse reality.
Your brain doesn't know
you're not the one
holding that grief,
falling in love,
walking through that door.

It says:
"This is real enough."

And so it adapts.
Builds bridges
between thought and feeling,
self and other.

This isn't escape.
It's return.
To feeling.
To meaning.
To self.

Chapter 7: Imagination Is a Muscle

Fiction doesn't stay on the page—it lives inside us. When we read a story, we're not simply following a plot. We're activating memory, imagination, emotion, and even physical sensation.

Fiction mirrors how memory works: not as a sterile recording of events, but as reconstruction, woven through emotion, meaning, and imagination.

When we read, we naturally fill in the gaps, imagining tone, gestures, smells, scenery. We co-create the experience based on our own emotional memory. That's why no two people read the same book in the same way. Our minds bring our selves to the story. And in doing so, we strengthen both memory and imagination—two of the deepest pillars of our humanity.

Stories are not imagined in theory. They are lived in feeling. They leave imprints not just in the memory but in the chest, the breath, and the very structure of the self.

Fiction as Emotional Rehearsal and Healing

Fiction offers a safe, contained space where we can encounter sorrow, anger, hope, and forgiveness without judgment or urgency.

Trauma researchers have found that narrative fiction helps the brain reprocess difficult emotions and build psychological resilience over time.

When we encounter grief, betrayal, and redemption on the page, our minds learn to hold these states better in real life. And our nervous systems—so often frayed by urgency and overload—begin to regulate, recalibrate, and restore.

Fiction doesn't fix us. It accompanies us. And sometimes, that is the truest form of healing.

Imagination: Not a Luxury, but a Lifeline

In a culture obsessed with productivity, imagination often gets dismissed as frivolous. But neuroscience tells a different story.

In *Imagination: The Science of Your Mind's Greatest Power*, cognitive scientist Jim Davies outlines why imagination is essential for survival:

1. It allows us to rehearse dangers before they happen.
2. It stretches us into compassion for lives we've never lived.
3. It helps us gently reframe and heal the past.
4. It preserves meaning when the world feels unrecognizable.

Imagination, in other words, is resilience in its softest, most powerful form. And fiction, by inviting us to imagine richly and tenderly, keeps that resilience alive.

Imagination Is How We Change

Psychologists and neuroscientists now recognize that imagination is key to creating change. Before we can live a new story, we must first be able to imagine it.

Dr. Joe Dispenza teaches that the brain cannot create a new future while anchored to the emotions of the past. To change our lives, we must imagine a different reality—and feel it as if it were already true. This begins to rewire the brain's circuitry and create new maps of possibility.

Fiction rehearses this same miracle. When we enter a story—when we hope with the character, fear with them, rejoice with them—we are practicing emotional transformation. We are reminding our brain that other outcomes exist, that pain isn't the only narrative. That love, resilience, and redemption are still possible.

Even if we don't yet believe we deserve more, fiction does. It holds hope for us when we've forgotten how to hold it ourselves. And through each imagined journey, we slowly strengthen the part of us that can dare to dream again.

For the Woman Who Has Stopped Dreaming
This chapter is for her. The woman who used to daydream but now only ticks boxes. The woman who used to imagine new beginnings but now only sees what must be endured.

If you feel numb, or stuck, or quietly resigned, fiction may feel far away right now. Let it meet you gently. Let it crack a window inside you. Let it remind your tired mind that not all stories end the way they begin. Some start again. And so can you.

Final Thought
Fiction is not indulgence. Fiction is resilience, rehearsed tenderly—page by page, neuron by neuron, heart by heart.

Every time you pick up a novel, you are not escaping. You are building the capacity to live your own story—with more breath, more beauty, and more belief.

Fiction and Stress: The Six-Minute Reset

We live in a world that rewards hustle, glorifies productivity, and floods us with constant stimulation. Stress becomes our baseline—so familiar, we barely notice it anymore.

But here's what science tells us: reading fiction can reduce stress by *68%* in just six minutes.

That's according to researchers at the University of Sussex, who found that participants who read silently for only a few minutes experienced a greater drop in stress than those who listened to music, drank tea, or went for a walk.

Why does fiction work so well?

Because it offers focused immersion—without pressure. It draws us into a coherent, emotionally rich narrative that gently interrupts the loop of worry. We're not escaping life. We're returning to our breath, our presence, our emotional center.

The imagination becomes a sanctuary. The nervous system softens. The mind slows. The body remembers calm.

Six minutes. A single page. A few well-chosen words. That's all it takes to begin coming back to yourself.

Chapter 8: When Stories Are Too Powerful to Silence

If fiction were meaningless, it wouldn't be feared. But around the world, stories are still being silenced—because they give voice to the unseen, power to the marginalized, and reflection to those who've been told they don't belong. The banned books that follow are not dangerous because they harm; they're dangerous because they heal. And healing is always a radical act.

Banned Books and the Quiet Revolution of Fiction

There is something quietly astonishing about the fact that, in a world filled with noise and conflict, it is still stories—simple ink on paper—that some fear most.

Books are still challenged. Still banned. Still labelled dangerous. Not because they wield weapons but because they wield something even harder to control: imagination, empathy, emotional awakening, belief.

Why Some Stories Are Feared

Across history, books have been banned, censored, or challenged for daring to question authority, break social taboos, or offer new ways of seeing the world. And, time after time, the stories silenced are the ones society needed most.

When a novel is banned, it's rarely because it poses true harm. It's because it threatens a certain kind of order—the kind of order that depends on silence, sameness, and obedience.

Books are often banned for confronting themes that challenge comfort or convention:

Political dissent (*1984, Animal Farm*)

Moral or religious taboos (*The Handmaid's Tale*)

Racial and social injustice (*To Kill a Mockingbird, The Hate U Give*)

Sexuality and identity (*The Color Purple, Fun Home*)

Honest depictions of life's complexity (*The Catcher in the Rye, Of Mice and Men*)

The truth behind most book bans isn't about protecting readers. It's about control—about shaping what is seen, what is said, and, ultimately, what is *believed*.

A Lineage of Courage: Stories that Endured

Many of the books that once caused outrage are now seen as essential literature:

Uncle Tom's Cabin fueled the abolitionist movement.

1984 became a warning against propaganda and authoritarianism.

I Know Why the Caged Bird Sings gave voice to trauma and resilience.

The Color Purple expanded conversations around race, gender, and survival.

Beloved forced readers to confront historical wounds too often buried.

Each of these novels pushed against the boundaries of their time—and changed what came after. Their very existence reminds us that it is not hatred that gets banned. It's *reckoning*. It's *truth*. It's the story of becoming more than the world says you're allowed to be.

Fiction as Quiet Resistance

When I first stumbled across a book on banned fiction tucked away on a small bookstore table—right next to a book on bibliotherapy—it was as if the pieces of my own journey clicked into place.

It's no accident that fiction heals. It's no accident that fiction transforms. And it's no accident that fiction scares those who profit from keeping people small.

Stories don't heal by fixing us. They heal by restoring our inner landscape, giving us mirrors for our strength, maps for our return to hope, and language for the grief we were never meant to carry alone.

To ban a book is to ban a possibility—that someone, somewhere, might read a story and realize: *I don't have to stay silent. I don't have to stay small.*

Why Banned Books Matter More than Ever

Today, book bans are rising again—often targeting stories about race, identity, history, and resilience. The need to protect and read these books is not just about literary freedom. It's about protecting the right to imagine a better world. Because banned books do more than provoke—they protect what matters:

1. They teach empathy.
2. They encourage critical thinking.
3. They preserve truth and memory.
4. They validate marginalized experiences.
5. They inspire personal and societal change.

Choosing to read a banned book isn't just an act of rebellion. It's an act of hope. It's a way of saying: "*I will not be afraid of truth. I will not be afraid of becoming more.*"

The Shelf as Sanctuary

Let your bookshelf be a quiet rebellion. Fill it with stories that ask hard questions. Stories that comfort *and* disrupt. Stories that remind you: courage can be as simple as turning the next page.

Fiction isn't dangerous because it lies. It's dangerous because it tells too much truth. And the world has always been changed by those willing to imagine it differently.

If you've ever been handed a story others tried to silence, hold it close. You've been entrusted with something sacred.

Book Friends
The most important "dangerous" books
Sometimes, the stories that are most challenged, most banned, and most feared are the ones that carry the greatest tenderness, courage, and truth. Below is a list of publications whose sale or availability was curtailed at some point in history.

For Political and Social Criticism
1984 by George Orwell
Often banned in authoritarian regimes, Orwell's chilling vision of surveillance and thought control remains one of the most powerful warnings about the erosion of truth and freedom. It reveals how language can be weaponized and how control can masquerade as order.

> ***Why it helps:*** Because it teaches us to question power, protect language, and defend emotional and intellectual freedom—before it's rewritten for us.

Fahrenheit 451 by Ray Bradbury
A novel about banning books—banned. Bradbury's classic reminds us that censorship rarely starts with fire; it begins with apathy. It is a timeless warning about the dangers of conformity and the fragility of knowledge.

> ***Why it helps:*** Because it reminds us that censorship starts with indifference, not passion. This novel reignites the reader's role as both witness and protector of truth.

Brave New World by Aldous Huxley
A provocative look at technology, pleasure, and societal control. Huxley imagines a world numbed by comfort and consumption, where individuality is sacrificed for the illusion of peace.

> *Why it helps:* Because it challenges us to examine comfort culture and the cost of emotional and intellectual numbness. It awakens the reader from passive distraction.

The Handmaid's Tale by Margaret Atwood
Banned for its political critique and depiction of gender oppression. Atwood's dystopia hits too close to home for many—which is exactly why it must be read. It imagines what happens when women's bodies become the battleground for ideology.

> *Why it helps:* Because it shows what happens when women's voices and bodies are controlled—and dares us to pay attention before fiction becomes reality.

Animal Farm by George Orwell
A political allegory critiquing totalitarianism through the lens of a farmyard uprising. Orwell's novella distills complex truths about propaganda, power, and betrayal in the simplest—and most enduring—language.

> *Why it helps:* Because it distills the complexity of power, betrayal, and revolution into a story that's hauntingly simple—and heartbreakingly familiar.

Stories That Address Race and Injustice
To Kill a Mockingbird **by Harper Lee**
Removed from schools for its language and uncomfortable truths about race. But its impact endures, helping readers of all ages confront injustice with conscience.

> *Why it helps:* Because it teaches courage through innocence and reveals the cost of complicity through silence. It reminds us that justice isn't abstract—it's deeply personal.

The Hate U Give **by Angie Thomas**
A powerful exploration of race, activism, and police violence in modern America. This novel gives voice to the grief and rage of a generation while offering hope through courage and community.

> *Why it helps:* Because it puts a face, a family, and a fierce voice to systemic injustice—and reminds us that change starts with story, spoken out loud.

For LGBTQ+
Gender Queer **by Maia Kobabe**
A deeply personal memoir in graphic novel form, exploring gender identity and expression. Kobabe's story has been widely banned, but its courage has opened doors for deeper conversations on nonbinary identity.

> *Why it helps:* Because it offers a mirror for those who've never seen themselves reflected—and a window for those ready to understand. This book normalizes the conversation with honesty and grace.

What They Tried to Silence

They banned it—
because it named the pain
too clearly.

Because it opened
a window too wide,
let in too much light,
or asked the reader
to question
what they'd been told
to believe.

They said it was dangerous.
But what they meant was:
It gave people
the language to rebel,
to weep,
to remember.

A banned book is
a bruised truth—
still breathing.
A mirror cracked
but not broken.

Read it anyway.
Let it rise again in your hands.
Let it say what someone else
was afraid you'd hear.

Chapter 9: The Mystery of a Sharper Mind

There's something undeniably satisfying about a good mystery. The puzzle. The pacing. The moment when a twist makes you pause and whisper, "Wait—what?"

But what you might not realize is this: When you're curled up with a mystery novel, your brain isn't just entertained; it's working out.

Mysteries aren't just fun. They're functional. They sharpen attention, improve memory, and help us think more critically. In fact, reading mystery fiction is one of the best things you can do to keep your mind agile, resilient, and—quite literally—young.

Why We're Drawn to Mysteries

It's not just the thrill of the whodunit. It's deeper than that. We are wired to seek resolution, to make sense of chaos, to solve what doesn't make sense. Mystery novels give us a safe, contained space to do that. They invite our brains to ask: *What's missing? What matters? What's real?* And when the pieces come together, it's more than satisfying. It's soothing.

Science tells us that every time we solve a clue or have an "aha" moment while reading, our brains release dopamine—the feel-good chemical that boosts motivation, focus, and even emotional regulation. It's not just pleasurable; it's healing.

The Brain on Mysteries: A Workout in Disguise

Reading mysteries engages multiple areas of the brain at once. We remember clues, weigh motives, consider outcomes, and constantly revise our predictions. It's complex and immersive, and it builds mental stamina.

Research shows that mystery readers don't just enjoy the story—they strengthen the mind:

- Working memory, by tracking events and details
- Critical thinking, by analyzing motives and outcomes
- Emotional intelligence, by identifying with morally complex characters

And maybe most importantly, mysteries strengthen *resilience*. We walk with characters through uncertainty, through fear, through not knowing–and we keep turning the page. In a world that rarely offers clean answers, that's powerful.

Mysteries & Mental Health: The Gentle Distraction

There's something comforting about the order of a mystery. Even when the plot is dark or the themes are difficult, there's a pattern, a rhythm, a promise: this will make sense eventually. And that brings relief to the nervous system.

Mysteries offer what real life often doesn't: a sense of closure. Which is why reading them can actually help regulate anxiety. The brain finds coherence. The heart finds calm.

Why Mysteries Keep You Sharp

They make you pause. They make you think again. They challenge your certainty and build your flexibility. All of which helps foster what neuroscientists call *neuroplasticity*–the brain's ability to form new connections and adapt. In short: mystery novels are brain food. And they're delicious.

Book Friends

If you're looking for books that keep your mind sharp and your imagination engaged, here are some excellent mystery novels that will give your brain the workout it craves.

The Silent Patient by Alex Michaelides

A psychological thriller that pulls you in with every twist. When a woman murders her husband and then stops speaking, the reader is taken on a rollercoaster ride of clues, theories, and shocking revelations.

> *Why it helps:* Because it challenges you to decode silence, trace trauma, and question every assumption. It's a masterclass in perspective—and proof that what's unsaid often speaks the loudest.

The Woman in the Window by A.J. Finn

A psychological mystery where a woman who believes she has witnessed a crime must grapple with her own mind. The shifting perspectives and unreliable narrative will keep you on the edge of your seat while stimulating your cognitive and emotional responses.

> *Why it helps:* Because it plays with perception, memory, and reality—all while exploring mental health with nuance. This novel gently sharpens the cognitive and emotional complexity as you read.

In the Woods by Tana French

A layered, atmospheric mystery that combines a chilling investigation with deep psychological exploration. French's detailed storytelling and intricate plot twists keep readers mentally engaged from start to finish.

> *Why it helps:* Because it invites deep attention and asks you to sit with uncertainty. Its haunting atmosphere and layered narrative demand focus, empathy, and intellectual resilience.

And Then There Were None by Agatha Christie

A masterpiece of suspense and structure, this novel strands ten strangers on a remote island—each hiding secrets, each marked for justice. As the body count rises, so does the psychological intensity.

A brilliant lesson in how the mind searches for safety even when there's nowhere left to hide.

> *Why it helps:* Because it's a magnificent exercise in logic, pacing, and emotional suspense. It proves that the mind, when guided by story, becomes both detective and mirror.

Behind Closed Doors by B.A. Paris

A chilling psychological thriller that unravels the disturbing truth behind a seemingly perfect marriage. With mounting tension and a deeply unsettling premise, the story reveals how charm can be a mask—and how silence can be a survival strategy.

> *Why it helps:* Because it invites emotional discernment, strengthens intuition, and helps readers recognize the signs of coercion and control.

A Time to Kill by John Grisham

A brutal crime. A father's vengeance. A courtroom that becomes a battleground for race, justice, and retribution. Set in the deep South, this is Grisham's first—and arguably most searing—legal thriller.

> *Why it helps:* Because it asks unflinching moral questions in the face of heartbreak. For those who feel silenced by systems or judged for their anger, this novel offers a form of reckoning.

Why Mysteries Are Good for the Brain

In quiet stacks, where clues reside,
a mystery waits—go take that ride!
With candlesticks and secret codes,
in mansions, trains, and darkened roads.

There's Miss Scarlet, sly and slick,
and Colonel Mustard—always quick.
Poirot preens with perfect flair,
while Sherlock finds the unseen air.
Each twist you trace, each plot you chase,
is mental cardio—at your own pace.
No need for treadmills, planks, or squats,
just clever turns and cunning plots.

Your neurons fire, your focus stays,
as red herrings dance through shadowed haze.
Forget your reps—just turn the page,
and let your brain outsmart its cage.

So grab a whodunit, sharp and tight—
by morning's end, you'll think more bright.
With every twist, your thoughts align:
mysteries train the brilliant mind.

Chapter 10: Bibliotherapy

The Healing Power of Story

I'll be honest—when I first heard the word bibliotherapy, I had no idea what it meant. Despite a lifelong love of books—and chapters of my life where fiction had quietly kept me afloat—I had never encountered the term. It's still relatively unknown in Canada, though it's beginning to find its way into the public conversation. Quietly, steadily, it's gathering momentum—first in the UK, where stories have long been prescribed like medicine, and now increasingly in the United States, where therapists and community programs are turning to fiction as a form of emotional healing. Even here in Canada, glimmers are beginning to appear—psychiatrists curating reading lists for mood disorders, libraries offering stories not just for escape, but for support. It seems the world is remembering something ancient: that the right story doesn't just entertain us—it knows us, steadies us, and sometimes saves us.

When I started to explore it, something inside me lit up. Here it was: confirmation of what I had long felt in my bones. Fiction heals. It doesn't just distract us or pass the time. It grounds us. It strengthens us. It gives us back pieces of ourselves we didn't even know had gone quiet.

When I discovered *Bibliotherapy: The Healing Power of Reading* by Bijal Shah, it felt like finding a language my heart already knew. She defines bibliotherapy as:

"An art therapy that leverages the power of stories to heal. Its magic lies in the relationship formed between the reader and the writing—fiction or non-fiction, poetry or essay—and the reflection of the thoughts, feelings, observations, and lessons that the writing provokes, through a daily journaling practice ('literary journaling') or counselling."

What I love most about that definition is how it honours both parts of the experience: the story itself, and the reflection it invites.

A Small Note About this Book

While *The Fiction Fix* draws deeply from the spirit of bibliotherapy, it's not a clinical manual or a structured therapeutic tool. This book isn't a prescription pad. It's a companion. A celebration of the way in which fiction, poetry, and metaphor can become a lifeline.

You won't find therapeutic protocols here. But you *will* find stories that remind you of your own strength, softness, and sovereignty. If even one page in this book helps you breathe more easily, feel seen, or take one small step forward, then it has done what bibliotherapy, in its deepest spirit, hopes to do:

To offer healing. To offer belonging. To offer homecoming.

A Brief History of Healing Through Story

Long before it had a name, storytelling was medicine. The ancient Greeks called libraries "healing places for the soul." In Thebes, a library inscription once read: "Medicine for the mind."

Even then, people understood what modern neuroscience is only beginning to confirm: stories aren't luxuries. They're tools for survival. They help us–

- Process grief
- Navigate uncertainty
- Reconnect with meaning

The word *bibliotherapy* was first used in 1916 by Samuel McChord Crothers, who described a "literary clinic" where books could offer solace, strength, and a way through life's challenges.

One quiet pioneer was Sadie Peterson Delaney, a librarian who used books to help veterans heal from the psychological wounds of war. She believed deeply in matching the right story to the right soul.

The Gifts of Bibliotherapy

You don't need a diagnosis, a formal session, or even a plan. You only need one thing: a willingness to meet a story exactly where you are.

Fiction becomes a soft space for what the world doesn't always allow:

Permission to feel: Stories hold sadness, hope, and longing without needing to fix or explain.

Companionship in the dark: Characters remind us that we are not alone.

Language for the unspoken: Stories often name what we've only felt.

A gentle rehearsal space: Fiction lets us practice courage and resilience in safe terrain.

A place to rest: In a world that worships productivity, fiction gives us permission to simply be.

A bridge back to ourselves: Page by page, we come home to who we are.

Healing doesn't always announce itself. Sometimes, it arrives quietly—between sentences, within metaphors, in the pause between paragraphs.

Creating Your Own Healing Library

You don't need a structured toolkit to begin. Just ask yourself—

What am I feeling right now?

What might I need to hear?

What kind of story would feel like company?

Then let your instinct choose. Pick a novel, a poem, or a story that feels right—even if you can't explain why. Let it walk beside you. And when the words stir something in you, let that be enough.

Healing is not a straight line. It's a spiral, a thread, a quiet remembering. And stories can be the hand that holds the thread.

Chapter 11: Listening is Reading

There are seasons when holding a book feels like too much. When the eyes are tired, the mind full, the hands busy. When concentration is scattered, or grief is loud, or the body simply asks to rest. In those seasons, many stop reading—not because they've lost the love of story, but because life has made it harder to sit still, to focus, to stay.

But story, if we let it, has a way of finding its way back in. It may not be through a printed page. It may be through a voice. A voice that enters the room like a presence. That walks beside you while you do the dishes. That curls beside you while you lie still in the dark.

This is the quiet beauty of the audiobook. It doesn't ask you to stop everything. It doesn't ask for perfect focus. It simply asks you to *receive*.

The Return of the Oral Tradition

Long before we wrote stories down, we spoke them. Around fires. Beside sickbeds. On long walks between villages.

The human voice has always been a vessel for memory, meaning, and magic. To listen to a story is not lesser—it is ancient. It is how myths were passed. How children learned the shape of the world. How grief was carried. How wisdom survived.

When we listen, we join something older than ourselves. A thread that connects our modern ears to ancestral ones. And in today's world—where we are pulled in so many directions—listening may be the most *accessible* way to come back to story.

This Is Not Cheating

Let's name the quiet shame some readers carry: *"If I'm not holding a book, does it count?"* Yes. It counts.

Listening is not cheating. It is not a shortcut. It is not a lesser version of reading.

It is *reading through the body*. Through the breath. It is reading with your ears instead of your eyes. It is letting the story be delivered, not decoded. And for many people, it is the only way that story feels safe, available, or sustainable.

Neurodivergent readers. Busy caregivers. People recovering from illness. Those with visual impairment. Or simply—those in a moment of life where the page feels far away.

Listening meets you where you are.

The Intimacy of Being Read To

There is something uniquely tender about being read to. Especially as an adult.

A good narrator doesn't just read a story—they *inhabit* it. They lend breath and pause, rhythm and weight. They know when to soften and when to quicken, when to let a moment land and when to carry you forward.

It is a form of holding.

And for many of us, it reawakens something early and essential: the comfort of being told a story before bed. The safety of a trusted voice. The feeling of not having to hold the whole world on our own.

When you're listening to a story, you are no longer the one turning pages. You are the one being carried.

And that is its own kind of healing.

How Listening Serves the Journey

In times of transition, depletion, or quiet growth, we don't always need more stimulation. We need gentle presence. A steady thread. A voice that reminds us we are still connected. That's what audiobooks offer:

They let the story arrive without requiring more of you.

They allow for depth without demand.

They create moments of meaning in the middle of the ordinary—commutes, walks, showers, sleepless nights

And for those doing emotional work—grief, healing, reinvention—they offer companionship without pressure.

There is no test. No analysis. Only *resonance*. A sentence can still land in the body. A line can still awaken something in the heart. A story can still be a turning point—even when you never touched a page.

You Don't Have to Sit Still to Be Moved
So if you are in a chapter of your life where print feels distant—listen. Let a voice meet you where you are. Let a sentence follow you down the hallway. Let a story accompany your footsteps. Let literature live in your ears and move through your body until something in you shifts.

You don't have to sit still to be moved. You don't have to be still to be stiller. Because story, when offered through the human voice, can feel even more alive.

It becomes not just something you read—but something you walk beside. Something that walks beside *you*.

Book Friends
Not all audiobooks are created equal. A powerful story can lose its resonance with the wrong voice. The pacing might rush. The tone might falter. And sometimes, even the most beautiful prose can feel flat when not held with care.

But then, there are those narrators who carry the story – and carry *you* with it. They don't just read the words. They *hold the space*. They become the bridge between the page and your nervous system. The presence in the room. The guide walking beside you.

The audiobooks in this section are more than great stories – they are gentle, powerful introductions to what the listening experience can be at its best. Whether you're new to audiobooks or returning after time away, these voices offer a kind of sanctuary. A place to begin again. A way to be read to, in the most sacred sense.

The Paper Palace written by MirandaCowleyHeller (narrated by Julia Whelan)

A woman spends one day at her family's summer home—revisiting the past, confronting a childhood trauma, and deciding whether to stay in her marriage or follow a long-buried love.

A story about memory, secrecy, and the split-second choices that shape a life. Julia's voice is both intimate and intelligent. She reads like someone who understands the *underneath* of a story—the grief hidden in breath, the tenderness in hesitation.

> ***Why it helps:*** Because it reminds us how deeply the past can live in the present – and how truth, even when buried, never really disappears. It invites us to reflect on the courage it takes to choose a different ending, even when everything is already in motion.

Jane Eyre by Charlotte Brontë (narrated by Thandiwe Newton)

An orphaned girl grows into a fiercely independent woman, navigating love, morality, and self-respect within a society that seeks to silence her. A timeless tale of resilience, romantic tension, and the quiet strength of a woman who refuses to disappear.

Thandiwe's voice is elegant, textured, and quietly powerful. She brings timeless stories into sharp emotional focus with grace and intelligence.

> ***Why it helps:*** Because it honors the integrity of a woman who listens to her inner knowing—no matter the cost. Jane's story is a reminder that self-respect can be its own form of liberation.

Crow Lake by Mary Lawson (narrated by Catherine McGregory)

In rural northern Ontario, a young girl grows up in the shadow of family tragedy and quiet sacrifice. A gentle, haunting novel about what we inherit, what we bury, and how childhood echoes across a lifetime.

Catherine narrates with a gentle clarity and a voice that feels rooted in landscape and emotion. Her work is often paired with Canadian literary fiction that explores memory, family, and identity.

> *Why it helps:* Because it gives voice to the grief we carry long after the moment has passed—and offers a tender, unhurried space to reflect on the patterns we unconsciously repeat. It's a soft invitation to feel what was never fully felt.

The Marrow Thieves by Cherie Dimaline (narrated by Michelle St. John)

In a dystopian future where Indigenous people are hunted for their bone marrow, which holds the key to dreaming, a group of survivors journeys toward safety and cultural reclamation. A visionary tale of survival, storytelling, and the sacred power of memory.

An award-winning Indigenous Canadian actor and voice artist, Michelle brings grounded intensity to everything she narrates. Her performance carries cultural wisdom, emotional power, and fierce protection.

> *Why it helps:* Because it restores dignity to Indigenous voices, and reminds us that memory is not just personal—it's collective, ancestral, and worth protecting. It teaches that even in a broken world, hope can still carry forward on foot, on story, and on soul.

The Fall of Gondolin by J.R.R. Tolkien
(Narrated by Timothy West & Samuel West)

The rise and ruin of a secret Elven city, betrayed from within and besieged by darkness—yet from its fall, a spark of future hope is carried forth. A mythic, mournful story of courage, collapse, and the grace that endures through legend and lineage.

With epic narration and rich musical interludes, this audiobook transforms Tolkien's mythic tale into a living, breathing experience. The Wests bring gravitas and emotional depth to every line, giving voice to one of Middle-earth's most poignant and beautiful tragedies.

> ***Why it helps:*** Because it reminds us that even in stories of collapse, grace can survive. That what is lost may still leave behind something sacred. And that the voice of a storyteller can carry us through sorrow into remembrance—and from remembrance, into hope.

Why Reading Fiction Matters

We slow down.
Fiction invites us to pause. To be present. To step out of the rush and back into reflection. In doing so, we soothe an overstimulated nervous system and restore our fractured attention.

We build emotional resilience.
By walking with characters through loss, love, change, and challenge, we gain insight into our own emotional landscapes—and emerge more prepared to meet life as it is.

We grow in empathy.
Fiction lets us step inside other lives. It softens judgment, deepens compassion, and reminds us that everyone is carrying something unseen.

We feel less alone.
The right book becomes more than a story—it becomes a companion. One that whispers, *"You're not the only one."*

We reconnect with imagination.
Stories wake up the creative mind. They make room for new possibilities when we feel stuck—and gently help us reimagine what might be.

We process our emotions.
Fiction gives language to what we can't always say. Grief, fear, longing, and hope find a safe place to rise, soften, and settle.

We rediscover forgotten parts of ourselves.
The child who read under the covers. The dreamer. The seeker. The part of us that quietly hoped. Fiction brings them back.

We remember joy.
Reading for pleasure is a kind of nourishment. It reminds us that beauty doesn't have to be earned, and that delight is reason enough.

We strengthen the brain.
Neuroscience confirms what readers have long known: fiction boosts memory, focus, empathy, and imagination—more effectively than nonfiction in many cases.

We feel more whole.
In a world that can fragment us, fiction helps us come home. Thought by thought. Page by page.

And somewhere between the first sentence and the last page, we remember who we are.

This Is How We Return

They say you're running away.
That fiction is a crutch.
That you're hiding from the world
because you can't handle it.

But what they don't understand
is that sometimes
the only way to survive reality
is to step outside of it for a while.

Escapism isn't weakness.
It's recovery.

It's what happens
when the mind
builds itself a small, quiet room
where no one is shouting
and everything broken
can stay broken
until you're ready to begin again.

Fiction is not denial.
It's rehearsal.
It's rest.
It's re-entry on your own terms.

When you lose yourself in a novel,
you're not disappearing–
you are gathering.

*A room where grief can breathe
and hope can return*

Part III:
Stories as Sanctuary

There are moments in life
when we don't need more advice—
we need a place to rest.

Stories have always offered that place.
A soft chair for the soul.
A room where grief can breathe,
laughter can rise,
and hope can return—quietly.

This section is for the stories that soothe.

Chapter 12: Fiction as Refuge

There are times when the world feels overwhelming—too intense, too loud. In those moments, even the bravest heart needs a place to rest. Fiction provides that place.

Not by ignoring what's real or pretending sorrow or fear aren't there, but by offering a sanctuary where your spirit can breathe, even as life asks too much. A novel becomes a quiet room you can step into, where grief can soften, hope can spark, and the tired parts of you can be held without judgment.

Stories have always been our shelter. Long before self-help manuals or therapy apps, there were characters who showed us how to endure, how to imagine, how to begin again.

Escapism Isn't Avoidance—It's Recovery

Escapism is often misunderstood. It's not avoidance—it's renewal. Avoidance numbs or denies what needs to be faced. Escapism, when practiced mindfully through fiction, creates the emotional space we need to rest, reflect, and return stronger.

Fiction invites us into other worlds—not to abandon our own, but to reset our nervous system, to shift our perspective, and to feel something deeply without being overwhelmed by it.

This is not running away. It's how we gather ourselves to keep going.

How Fiction Helps Us Recover
Provides a Mental Reset
Fiction lets us step away from daily stressors without disconnecting from meaning. It engages the imagination while offering structured emotional relief.

Offers Emotional Processing Through Story
Sometimes, we can't face emotions head-on. But through fictional characters, we gently feel what we've been carrying. Their stories help us metabolize our own.

Encourages Hope and Perspective
Even in dark chapters, fiction reminds us that light returns. That healing is possible. That endings can hold new beginnings.

A Room Made of Story
In a world that rarely pauses, where notifications ping endlessly and the pace of life can feel relentless, a novel is more than a pastime. It's a doorway. A breath. A sanctuary.

Stories have always been places of refuge. Long before therapists, algorithms, or mindfulness apps, we found shelter in the rhythm of words. They remind us of who we are, who we've been, and who we're still becoming. But in a world designed to fragment our attention, we must now choose to make space for fiction. We must decide to slow down, to soften, to sit with story.

This is your invitation to build a sanctuary of stories—one that lives not just on your bookshelf but in your body, your breath, your daily rhythm.

Why Stories Need Space
We create rituals for wellness: sleep, movement, meditation. Why not stories?

Reading is not idle. It is active restoration. A single chapter can lower your stress levels, regulate your breath, and return you to yourself. But for that to happen, we need to approach fiction as more than something "extra." We must give it presence, and presence requires space.

Creating Your Sanctuary
A story sanctuary isn't about a picture-perfect reading nook. It's about reclaiming reading as a form of nourishment and honouring it with care:

Claim a corner: A favourite chair, a sunny patch on the floor, a bed warmed by tea and quiet. Let your body learn: this is where the world slows down.

Make it a ritual: Read while your coffee brews, after work, before sleep, in the soft spaces between tasks. Let it be a return, not a reward.

Curate a shelf: Build a collection that feels like home. Books you've loved. Books you long for. Books that hold parts of you that you haven't yet named.

Let fiction meet you where you are: You don't need to finish every book. You don't need to read what others love. Let go of the "shoulds." Follow resonance.

Try different forms: Audio, poetry, short stories, even graphic novels—fiction wears many faces. What matters is not format but feeling.

Closing Reflection

Not every act of healing is loud. Sometimes, it looks like sitting quietly with a book in your lap and your hand on your heart. In these soft moments—when you let the world slip away and step into someone else's shoes—you're not escaping.

You're recovering. Recalibrating. Returning.

Fiction offers more than story. It offers stillness. It offers sanctuary. And in a world that so often demands we hurry, achieve, and prove, the simple act of turning a page becomes revolutionary.

So, rest here. Let the story do its quiet work. Let beauty hold you where logic can't. And when you're ready, carry that softness with you back into the world.

Book Friends

Some books don't just entertain—they soothe. They hold us gently when the world feels too sharp, and they remind us that we are not alone in what we carry. Whether you're looking for emotional healing, nostalgic comfort, or simply a story to curl up with, these novels offer quiet restoration. Let them meet you where you are.

Let these stories be your refuge. Let them remind you that healing doesn't have to be loud. Sometimes, all it takes is a quiet chapter and a moment to breathe.

The Little Paris Bookshop by Nina George

A literary apothecary prescribes novels for the heartbroken, the weary, and the lost. A gentle, sensory celebration of books as medicine.

> *Why it helps:* Because it affirms what we already know: stories can heal. This one wraps you in scent, soul, and softness.

Tara Road by Maeve Binchy

When two women—one in Dublin, one in Connecticut—unexpectedly swap homes for the summer, their lives begin to shift in quiet, life-altering ways. Through new surroundings and unexpected friendships, each begins to heal from personal loss and rediscover a sense of self.

> *Why it helps:* Because it offers a tender, spacious kind of healing. The kind that unfolds slowly, through setting, connection, and self-forgiveness. Maeve Binchy reminds us that refuge doesn't always come through escape—it often arrives through perspective, and the courage to begin again.

The Very Secret Society of Irregular Witches by Sangu Mandanna

Mika Moon is a lonely witch hiding her magic in modern-day England, posting pretend spells online until she's unexpectedly hired to teach three young witches at a remote manor called Nowhere House. There, she finds eccentric caretakers, curious children, and one grumpy yet quietly tender librarian who doesn't believe in magic—until Mika's presence begins to change everything.

> *Why it helps:* Because it blends cozy charm with quiet transformation. This is a feel-good novel about belonging, found family, and soft, late-blooming love, wrapped in just enough magic to remind us that being different can be our greatest gift.

Garden Spells by Sarah Addison Allen

In the small Southern town of Bascom, North Carolina, the Waverley sisters have inherited more than just a crumbling family home. Their garden is enchanted—its plants infused with mysterious properties, its apples said to reveal the biggest moment of your life. When estranged sister Sydney returns home with a daughter in tow, old wounds stir, but so does the quiet magic of belonging.

> *Why it helps:* Because it blends the soft ache of family with the lush wonder of everyday magic. This novel is an ode to second chances, sisterhood, and the hidden ways in which the world conspires to help us bloom again.

Miss Benson's Beetle by **Rachel Joyce**
In 1950s England, Margery Benson shocks everyone—most of all herself—by abandoning her gray routine to chase a childhood dream: finding a mythical golden beetle in the wilds of New Caledonia. Accompanied by Enid Pretty, a wildly inappropriate assistant in cherry red lipstick, she sets off on an absurd, dangerous, and unexpectedly soul-deep adventure.

> *Why it helps:* Because it reminds us that reinvention isn't reserved for the young. This story is a whimsical testament to the healing power of friendship, risk, and the strange, beautiful things that happen when we follow our curiosity—even late in life.

The Girl Who Circumnavigated Fairyland in a Ship of Her Own Making by **Catherynne M. Valente**
Twelve-year-old September is spirited away from her ordinary life in Omaha to the wild, whimsical world of Fairyland, where she must retrieve a witch's spoon, befriend a book-loving wyvern, and challenge a fickle marquess. Told in rich, lyrical prose, this modern fairy tale is equal parts clever, courageous, and deeply enchanting.

> *Why it helps:* Because it reminds us that adventure lives inside imagination. This novel is for the inner child who once longed for the fantastical—and the grown woman who still needs to be reminded that she can build her own ship, her own story, and her own way home.

Howl's Moving Castle by **Diana Wynne Jones**
When Sophie is cursed into becoming an old woman, she stumbles into the chaotic, magical world of the wizard Howl and his unpredictable moving castle. What follows is a riotous adventure

filled with spells, sass, and unexpected friendships. With wit and warmth, this story celebrates self-discovery, transformation, and the magic that finds us when we least expect it.

> *Why it helps:* Because whimsy heals. This novel reminds us that even when everything feels out of control, joy, enchantment, and courage can still bloom—often in the most unlikely places.

The Night Circus by **Erin Morgenstern**

Le Cirque des Rêves appears without warning—an otherworldly circus of black-and-white tents, open only at night. Within its gates, two illusionists, bound by a magical competition, create breathtaking wonders that blur the line between performance and enchantment. But as their rivalry deepens, so does a quiet, impossible love that's woven into the fabric of the circus itself.

> *Why it helps:* Because it offers a sensory escape into wonder. This novel invites you to slow down, exhale, and step into a world of quiet magic, beauty, and mystery—where imagination becomes a balm for the weary spirit.

The Garden of Angels by **David Hewson**

A quiet, heartwarming novel set in post-WWII Venice, where a young girl's kindness leaves a lasting legacy. A moving story of love, resilience, and community.

> *Why it helps:* Because it reminds us that even in times of ruin, kindness plants roots that last. A gentle echo of how hope can grow quietly, even in the darkest soil.

The Four Winds by **Kristin Hannah**
Set during the Dust Bowl, this novel follows one woman's fierce determination to survive. A story of endurance, motherly love, and hard-won hope.

> ***Why it helps:*** Because it honors quiet strength and stubborn hope. This story reminds us that what we endure can shape–not break–who we are.

The Keeper of Lost Things by **Ruth Hogan**
A tender tale about memory, loss, and the small magic of everyday kindness. Each found object holds a story–and each story helps someone heal.

> ***Why it helps:*** Because it shows us how ordinary things can hold extraordinary meaning. This novel brings comfort by honouring the quiet power of connection.

The Reading List by **Sara Nisha Adams**
A touching story about how books bring unlikely people together. Heartfelt, relatable, and a celebration of how shared stories can bridge generations.

> ***Why it helps:*** Because it affirms the healing power of shared stories and reminds us that books can be bridges between souls, generations, and life's lonely moments.

The Lost and Found Bookshop by **Susan Wiggs**
A grieving woman finds her way back to life through the dusty

aisles of her family's bookshop. A story about second chances, love, and healing.

> *Why it helps:* Because it offers comfort in grief and the hope of starting over, and a gentle nudge that healing often begins with one small, brave step.

Remarkably Bright Creatures by Shelby Van Pelt

A charming novel about grief, redemption, and an unlikely friendship with a highly intelligent octopus. Whimsical, poignant, and quietly uplifting.

> *Why it helps:* Because it makes space for grief without drowning in it. This story reminds us that connection—however unexpected—can rescue us.

The Guernsey Literary and Potato Peel Pie Society by Mary Ann Shaffer & Annie Barrows

Told in letters, this novel captures friendship, survival, and the power of storytelling in the wake of WWII. Warm, witty, and unforgettable.

> *Why it helps:* Because it reminds us that community and words can save us. A testament to the human spirit wrapped in humour and heart.

The Music Shop by Rachel Joyce

A vinyl record store owner uses music to heal the hearts of his customers—and maybe even his own. A tender story of connection and quiet transformation.

Why it helps: Because it speaks to the quiet healing power of art. This novel is a melody of comfort for anyone who's ever needed a second chance.

The Library of Lost and Found by Phaedra Patrick

A reclusive librarian discovers a mysterious book that changes everything she thought she knew about her past.

Why it helps: Because it honours the stories we carry—and the ones waiting to be written. This novel is a quiet nudge toward courage, connection, and reclaiming your narrative.

Nostalgic Comfort Reads

The Enchanted April by Elizabeth von Arnim

Four very different English women, each feeling unfulfilled or invisible in her own life, impulsively rent an Italian villa for the month of April. Amid blooming wisteria and sunlit terraces, transformation unfolds—not just through beauty but through companionship, silence, and unexpected self-renewal.

Why it helps: Because it offers a sun-drenched escape into possibility. This novel is a soft exhale—an invitation to believe in personal renewal, chosen joy, and the healing power of stepping away from one life to glimpse another.

Miss Buncle's Book by D.E. Stevenson

Faced with financial trouble during the Depression era, shy and unassuming Barbara Buncle writes a novel under a pen name—one that satirizes her quaint English village. The book becomes a runaway hit... but chaos ensues when her neighbors begin to recognize themselves in its pages.

> *Why it helps:* Because it's a reminder that quiet women can stir up real change. Full of charm, whimsy, and understated wit, this novel is a nostalgic escape into a gentler time, where imagination saves the day and happiness unfolds in the most unexpected ways.

Emily of New Moon by L.M. Montgomery

Often overshadowed by Anne Shirley, Emily Byrd Starr is the quieter, more introspective heroine of Montgomery's imagination. A budding writer with a strong will and mystical sensitivity, Emily navigates grief, girlhood, and the pull of creativity in a world that doesn't always understand her.

> *Why it helps:* Because it honours the strange and tender child in all of us. This story is for the dreamers, the diary-keepers, the ones who felt different—and who grew into that difference with grace. A nostalgic balm for quiet strength and imaginative resilience.

The Storied Life of A.J. Fikry by Gabrielle Zevin

A lonely bookseller's life is changed by an unexpected visitor and the rediscovery of love, joy, and purpose through story. As the chapters of his life unfold, he finds that even loss can lead to unexpected beginnings.

> *Why it helps:* Because it reminds us that lives—like books—can be rewritten. A warm, affirming tale of healing through connection.

The Bookshop on the Corner by Jenny Colgan

An out-of-work librarian opens a mobile bookshop in a Scottish village. As books find their readers and hearts begin to mend, this story becomes a love letter to second chances and the magic of finding your place. A delightful tale of reinvention, courage, and community.

> *Why it helps:* Because it gently affirms the power of starting again. A quiet joy for anyone who's ever dreamed of a softer life.

The Shell Seekers by Rosamunde Pilcher

A sweeping family saga that unfolds with depth, heart, and grace. Pilcher's storytelling is like a warm cup of tea for the soul. With its intergenerational perspective and quiet emotional revelations, this novel wraps you in the comfort of homecoming and hindsight.

> *Why it helps:* Because it reminds us that love and memory live in layers. A tender invitation to reflect, soften, and savor.

The Lark Rise to Candleford Trilogy by Flora Thompson

A nostalgic and beautifully observed portrait of English village life, full of gentle detail, quiet wisdom, and timeless grace. Through young Laura's eyes, we witness the rhythms of a changing world—one rooted in tradition yet gently moving toward modernity. The trilogy weaves the simplicity of rural life with tender reflections on memory, belonging, and the passage of time.

> *Why it helps:* Because it is peace on the page. A return to slowness, community, and stories that ask for nothing but attention.

She Opened the Book to Disappear

She opened the book
not to study,
not to strive—
but to disappear.

Not forever—
just long enough
to remember
the feel of stars
beneath her skin.

To walk through wardrobes
and forgotten gardens,
to sit beside wizards
and wide-eyed girls
who carried magic
like lanterns
in their chests.

She wasn't running away—
she was running *toward*
the part of herself
that still believed
in keys, and doors,
and love that waits
on the other side.

Chapter 13: The Quiet Medicine of Laughter

Laughter may not be listed on a doctor's prescription pad. But it is, in every way, a kind of medicine. Quiet. Subtle. Often unexpected. But powerful. Not the forced kind. Not the kind that masks pain or dismisses depth. But the kind that sneaks in like sunlight through heavy curtains. The kind that reminds us we're still alive. That joy is not gone—it's just been quiet, waiting for its moment to return.

In a world that feels increasingly serious, urgent, and heavy, humour can feel almost defiant: a radical reclaiming of levity, and a reminder that the soul was never meant to carry the weight of the world without relief.

We don't laugh to escape the truth. We laugh to survive it. To soften it. To carry it differently.

When we read fiction that makes us smile—really smile—it creates space in our chest, in our body, and in our soul.

Humour lowers cortisol. It relaxes the nervous system. It helps us exhale. It rebalances. It rewires. It restores.

And laughter, especially when it arises unexpectedly—between characters, in dialogue, in a delightfully absurd twist—does something even more important: It brings us back to ourselves. Not the weary, overwhelmed version, but the one underneath. The one that remembers joy. The one that still knows how to play.

Some novels do this gently, with wit and charm. Others do it boldly, with satire, mischief, or delightfully irreverent truth-telling. But all of them give us permission to remember that healing isn't always solemn. Sometimes, it sounds like laughter echoing through the quiet of a hard day.

So, let this chapter be your invitation to smile again, laugh again, and rediscover the medicine you may not have realized you needed. Because laughter is not the absence of grief. It's the breath that carries you through it.

Book Friends

Let these books lift you gently. Let them remind you that laughter is not only allowed on the healing path—it belongs there.

The Rosie Project by Graeme Simsion

Don Tillman is a brilliant but socially awkward professor who approaches love like a science experiment. What follows is equal parts hilarious and heartfelt. Beneath the laughs is a tender exploration of difference, vulnerability, and what it means to open our hearts anyway.

> *Why it helps:* Because it's a reminder that love isn't a formula. This story helps us laugh at ourselves while holding space for neurodiversity, awkwardness, and the courage it takes to truly connect.

The 100-Year-Old Man Who Climbed Out of the Window and Disappeared by Jonas Jonasson

This tale of an elderly man escaping his nursing home and embarking on an unexpected adventure offers both belly laughs and sharp reflections on history, aging, and freedom.

> *Why it helps:* Because joy doesn't expire. This novel reminds us that age is not a cage and that playfulness, rebellion, and renewal are always within reach.

Anita de Monte Laughs Last by Xochitl Gonzalez

Smart, biting, and deeply observant, this novel blends satire with feminist insight. It pokes at the pretensions of art, academia, and social power while lifting up the voices of women who have been overlooked—and aren't laughing quietly anymore.

> *Why it helps:* Because sometimes laughter is a form of justice. This novel is a rallying cry disguised as wit, restoring voice and dignity through sharp, necessary humor.

The Fun Times Brigade by Lindsay Zier-Vogel
A group of misfits—each with burdens and quirks of their own—find unexpected joy in one another's company.

> *Why it helps:* Because joy is often found in the unexpected. This story affirms that healing doesn't always look dramatic—sometimes, it's simply being welcomed as you are.

Nothing to See Here by Kevin Wilson
A hilarious and strangely touching novel about a woman who ends up caring for two children who spontaneously burst into flames when upset. Underneath the absurdity is a raw, moving look at parenting, outsiderhood, and unconditional love.

> *Why it helps:* Because absurdity can hold truth. This novel gently asks us to see beauty in the unpredictable and to love the parts of ourselves—and others—that sometimes feel uncontainable.

The Cactus by Sarah Haywood
Susan Green has her life under tight control—logical, efficient, emotionally distant. But an unexpected pregnancy and the death

of her mother challenge her carefully constructed world. As she navigates grief, family tension, and the strange tenderness of unexpected friendship, Susan's rigid world slowly begins to soften.

> ***Why it helps:*** Because it reminds us that even the prickliest people hold deep reservoirs of feeling, and that transformation often arrives disguised as disruption.

The Kindest Sound

Laughter is often seen as the opposite of sorrow—but sometimes, it's the companion. The breath that returns after we've held it too long. The exhale that says, "I'm still here." The music that rises in us when the heaviness finally lifts—even just a little.

We don't laugh because everything is fine. We laugh because something inside us remembers lightness. Remembers joy. Remembers that even in the deepest grief, the soul is still capable of delight.

Let humour be a bridge back to yourself. Let it surprise you. Let it soften what has grown too sharp. And when it finds you— whether as a giggle, a grin, or a belly-deep roar— let it be medicine. Let it be grace. Let it be enough.

The Quiet Medicine of Laughter

It doesn't always arrive
with sound.
Sometimes laughter is just
a soft lift in the chest,
a loosening in the shoulders,
a flicker of light
where heaviness had taken hold.

It sneaks in
through an unexpected line,
a character's awkward grace,
a moment so absurd
you can't help but smile.

Laughter doesn't erase the sorrow.
It simply reminds you,
you are still alive
beneath it.

And maybe—just maybe—
you're healing,
even now.
Even here.

Chapter 14: Why There Is Poetry Here

This is a book about fiction. But threaded through its pages, you will find poems—some long, some short, some whispered between chapters like breath between sentences.

Why? Because sometimes, a story needs a pause. A moment to let meaning settle. A space to feel what cannot be explained.

Fiction, for all its beauty, is structured: it arcs, it builds, it carries us from one place to another. Poetry is different. Poetry distills. It takes emotion and places it in the palm of your hand like a smooth stone. You may not know why it comforts you or how it got there—but somehow, it speaks.

This book carries many truths. Some are told in stories. Some needed the softness of a poem to land.

Poetry has always walked beside the soul. It is the language of lovers, mystics, exiles, and pilgrims. It comforts the dying, awakens the sleeping, and gives the grieving something to hold. Poetry doesn't ask for permission. It arrives in full bloom—often just when the heart needs it most.

It also plays a vital role in emotional recovery. It gives shape to feelings that are otherwise formless—grief, rage, awe, despair. When the mind is overwhelmed or the heart too full, a poem can be a lifeline. Not because it solves anything, but because it sees. It names. It allows.

In therapeutic circles, poetry is increasingly recognized not just as art but as medicine—for trauma survivors, caregivers, and those living through loss or transition. A single stanza can validate an entire season of sorrow. A few quiet lines can make the unbearable bearable. Poetry doesn't rescue us from pain. It walks with us through it.

When I began writing *The Fiction Fix*, I didn't plan to include poetry. I imagined essays. Research. Lists of recommended novels. But as I wrote, something deeper stirred. Certain stories wanted to be cradled, not catalogued. Certain memories asked to be sung, not summarized. And so, I began to write poems.

Some emerged from lived experience: grief, forgiveness, awe, endurance. Others came as whispers from something larger than me, as if the stories themselves wanted their own prayers.

The poems in this book are not decoration. They are doorways. They help the mind rest and the heart rise.

They are pauses, yes—but also portals.

The Ancient Thread

We have always needed poets. Before the printing press, before the novel, before the self-help shelves groaned with advice, we had verse. The Psalms. The Vedas. The Tao Te Ching. Epic chants around fires in forgotten forests. Poetry was how we prayed, how we remembered, how we survived.

Even now, in this modern world of algorithms and endless scrolls, we turn to poems at life's thresholds—at births, weddings, and funerals. At the edges of love and loss, prose often falters. Poetry does not. It steps forward with quiet strength and says, *"Here. Let me speak for you."*

In my own life, poetry has been both balm and compass. It has helped me understand what my intellect could not grasp and given shape to emotions that defied ordinary language.

Two poets in particular have been lifelong companions: Rumi and Khalil Gibran. Rumi speaks of longing and union, of turning toward the heart, of the Beloved within. His words invite us to remember what we already know deep in the bone— that love is both origin and destination. His poems do not shy away from pain; they honour it as a sacred threshold. Khalil Gibran writes with sacred stillness—tender, profound, deeply reflective. His prose-poems carry the hush of something ancient remembered. In his world, the soul is a house with many rooms, each emotion a visitor and each sorrow a sculptor of joy.

Each of these voices reminds me that to feel deeply is not weakness—it is a gateway. A doorway to beauty, connection, and truth.

What else is fiction if not an attempt to do the same? To remind us of our own astonishing light—even if we must travel through darkness to reach it?

An Invitation to Pause

Throughout this book, you will come upon a poem just when you need it. Sometimes, that poem will open a chapter. Sometimes, it will close one. A few will be given a page of their own—two-page spreads that act as breathing room between emotional terrains.

You don't need to analyze them. Poetry doesn't ask to be understood; it only asks to be felt. Let these poems be your quiet companions. Let them stand beside the stories. Let them whisper when the world grows too loud.

Book Friends

The Essential Rumi by Rumi (trans. Coleman Barks)

For the longing heart, the spiritual seeker, the one who dances at the edge of divine love.

> *Why it helps:* Because Rumi's poetry opens the soul through paradox, passion, and surrender. It dissolves separation and reminds us we are already part of the divine.

The Prophet by Khalil Gibran

For the philosopher of the heart who seeks wisdom wrapped in beauty and love expressed through luminous thought.

> *Why it helps:* Because Gibran's verses are medicine for the soul, distilling universal truths with grace, clarity, and eternal resonance.

Let the Poem Speak

Not every truth needs a paragraph.
Some arrive
as breath,
as ache,
as light across the floor
at the hour no one is watching.

A poem does not explain.
It remembers

It reminds.

Of what you lost.
Of what you carry.
Of what still waits to be found.

Let it rise,
this small sacred thing.
Let it say what prose cannot.
And when it finishes—
do not rush.

The silence that follows
is also part of the poem.

Chapter 15: Sanctuary in the Wild: Nature as Healer

There are sanctuaries made of stone and stained glass. And then, there are the older ones—made of wind, water, leaf, and sky.

Before we knew the word trauma, before we spoke of emotional regulation or nervous system recovery, there was the earth. It offered its stillness. It offered its rhythm. And it asked for nothing in return.

When I am working through grief, burnout, anxiety, or heartbreak, there is almost an instinctive pull toward nature. Not because I am looking for an answer, but because the forest doesn't talk back. The sky doesn't try to fix. Nature doesn't demand that we explain ourselves. It simply receives us as we are.

This isn't just poetic metaphor—it's a practice. In Japan, there is a widely respected healing modality called *shinrin-yoku*, or forest bathing. It involves immersing oneself in the atmosphere of the forest, not for exercise or achievement but for presence. No phone. No agenda. Just the quiet companionship of trees.

Research now shows that this kind of slow, mindful time in nature lowers cortisol levels, reduces anxiety, and restores emotional balance. Canada has begun to recognize its benefits as well, and forest therapy guides are now offering walks across the country. The medicine isn't a supplement—it's the woods themselves.

In many ways, forest bathing is a form of reading. It's reading the language of stillness. Of birdsong. Of dappled light and rustling branches. And it, too, reminds us that we belong.

In this way, nature is not only a sanctuary—it is a mirror. It reminds us that change is part of the cycle. That decay gives way to bloom. That stillness is not the absence of movement but the presence of peace. And that beauty can survive even the harshest winter.

Fiction rooted in the natural world has a similar effect. It slows the reader down, brings breath into the body, and returns us to something ancient inside ourselves—a knowing that cannot be named, only remembered.

The novels in this section are not about nature in a scientific sense. They are about the human spirit in conversation with the land. About healing that happens not through effort but through presence. They are stories that let you walk barefoot again—if only for a few pages.

Book Friends
The Overstory by **Richard Powers**
A sweeping, layered novel that reveals the interconnected lives of people and trees, reminding us that nature's story is also our own.

> *Why it helps:* Because it reawakens reverence. This novel expands our understanding of time, roots us in something greater, and calls us back to the wisdom of the living earth.

The Snow Child by **Eowyn Ivey**
Set in the Alaskan wilderness, this magical realist novel speaks to grief, hope, and the redemptive beauty of the natural world.

> *Why it helps:* Because it reminds us that even in frozen grief, something can bloom. Nature here becomes both mirror and balm—softening sorrow with wonder.

Prodigal Summer by **Barbara Kingsolver**
Three quietly intertwined stories unfold in the Appalachian mountains, celebrating nature's cycles and the unexpected ways in which we heal.

Why it helps: Because it honors the intelligence of the wild. This story shows how deeply the rhythms of nature live in us—and how returning to them can bring us back to ourselves.

Greenwood by Michael Christie

A sweeping multigenerational novel rooted in one family's bond with the forest, this is a moving exploration of environmental legacy, belonging, and the quiet strength passed down like rings in a tree.

Why it helps: Because it shows that healing is inherited. Through forest and family, this novel reminds us that the stories we carry—like trees—can survive, adapt, and shelter others.

The Bear by Andrew Krivak

In a post-apocalyptic future, a father and daughter are the last humans left. As the daughter comes of age in deep communion with the natural world, the novel becomes a quiet, meditative reflection on loss, resilience, and the sacredness of the earth.

Why it helps: Because it centres what we often forget: that we belong to the earth, not the other way around. This novel is a tender meditation on solitude, simplicity, and spiritual survival.

The Wild Knows

The wild does not ask
if you are worthy
of rest.

It does not count
your bruises
or your unfinished lists.

It says—
Come.

Come sit by the river.
Come watch the light.
Come be a thing
without a name
for a while.

And you do.
And you are.
And the wild,
in its silence,
sings you whole.

Healing begins at the threshold

Part IV:
Stories that Heal Us

Some stories arrive not to entertain –
but to mend.

This section begins with a guide,
because healing is not linear.
Readers will find what they need,
when they're ready.

Turn the page gently.

Your Survival Kit

You won't find it in the emergency aisle.
There's no flashlight.
No batteries.
No waterproof matches.

But it's there.
In the books
you've carried through
grief,
loneliness,
and the long nights
when hope felt out of reach.

It's there
in the stories that held your breath
when you couldn't hold your own.
In the characters
who said the thing
you didn't know
you needed to hear.

These are not just books.
They are bandages.
Beacons.
Benedictions.

You didn't call it healing.
You just called it reading.
But it kept you here.
Turning pages.
Finding light.

Every novel you've loved
has left something behind—
a piece of strength,
a new question,
a softening.

And all of it
has become your kit.
Not for emergencies alone—
but for life.
For the ordinary ache
and the extraordinary beauty
of being human.

So if you're wondering
what to pack for what's next—
Start here.

Take the books
that made you feel
less alone.
The ones that cracked you open
and handed you back your voice.

Your reading life
is not a hobby.

It's a shelter.
A compass.
A quiet kind of armor.

And you carry it with you
wherever you go.

Chapter 16: Stories that Heal Us

There are seasons in life when even hope feels out of reach. When the body aches, the family fractures, the nights stretch too long. When loss, loneliness, or illness seem to undo the very shape of who we are.

And sometimes, healing begins with a story. This section is a quiet place for those stories. Through the lens of fiction, we visit lives that hold what we may not yet have words for—grief, trauma, caregiving, estrangement, chronic pain, buried anger, unspoken need. Here, in these carefully chosen pages, fiction becomes more than escape. It becomes witness—and, sometimes, even balm.

Fiction Prescriptions

This is where the Fiction Prescriptions truly begin—not with solutions but with companionship. These are stories that sit with us in the silence. That walk with us through what cannot be fixed, only faced. Stories that whisper: *"You are not alone. And you are not beyond repair."*

Let this chapter be a threshold. A resting place. A page you turn to when you don't know what else to do—but still believe something true might meet you there.

How These Categories Were Chosen

The themes in this section weren't chosen by algorithms or popularity. They emerged slowly—like memories, or like truths waiting for language. Each one reflects a core emotional experience that many women face at some point in life—often silently.

They were drawn from real conversations. Coaching sessions. Friendships. Late-night worries. Personal losses. And the unspoken ache so many carry in the space between who they are and what the world asks them to be.

Some categories—like grief or trauma—are immediately recognizable. Others—like emotional silencing or imposter syndrome—may arrive more subtly, naming something a reader has long felt but never quite framed.

Together, these themes form a map of the inner terrain we walk as women: The pain we've endured; The identities we've outgrown or still long to claim; The caregiving we've done without applause; The quiet fears that edge our ambitions; The sacred longing to come home to ourselves.

Each section holds fiction chosen not just for its literary merit but for its emotional resonance. For its ability to name what hurts—and offer a mirror that says: *"You're not alone."* This is not about "fixing" our lives. It's about finding the right story to sit beside us as we live them.

Let these categories be doorways. Enter wherever you need to. Skip what doesn't serve you. Linger where something stirs.

These stories don't promise answers. But they do promise company. And sometimes, that's where healing begins.

Where Stories Meet Real Life

These are not just categories. They are lived experiences. Quiet heartbreaks. Lingering questions. Brave new chapters.

This list was created to help you find the stories that speak to your season—whether you're navigating grief, reclaiming your voice, or simply remembering that joy is still yours to hold.

You don't need to start at the beginning. You don't need to read it all. Just find the doorway that calls to you—and step through it.

Heartache & Healing
    Abuse (Abusive Relationships & Childhood Abuse)
    Addiction, Recovery & Return
    Recovering from Trauma
    Grief & loss
    Forgiveness (self & others)

Inner Struggles & Self-Perception
- Body image
- Self-worth & identity
- Imposter syndrome
- Mental wellbeing (anxiety, depression)
- Emotional silencing

Belonging & Disconnection
- Family dysfunction
- Isolation & loneliness
- LGBTQ+ rejection & the search for belonging

Life Transitions & Identity Shifts
- Motherhood
- Still vital—celebrating aging
- Finding purpose (post-retirement)
- Caregiving

Resilience & Renewal
- Burnout
- Resilience
- Chronic illness & disabilities
- Climate grief
- Fear, collective grief & world trauma
- Staying human in a cruel world

Section 1: Heartache & Healing

Some wounds arrive without warning.
Others are old companions
we've carried for years
in silence.

Loss.
Loneliness.
Pain that doesn't ask permission.
Love that left.
Or stayed—and changed.

This is not the chapter of easy answers.
This is the one where we
learn how to sit beside our ache
without being swallowed by it.

The stories here
know what it means
to lose your footing
and still get up.
To break—and soften,
not harden.

They do not rush the healing.
They hold space for it.
They remind us that
even in the deepest hurt,
we are not alone

Abuse

Naming What Was Never Yours to Carry

Abuse wears many faces. It may come from a partner's rage or from a parent's silence. It may arrive through control, neglect, or cruelty that was never called what it truly was.

Some of us were hurt by people who said they loved us. Some of us stayed far too long, while others were harmed before we even had the chance to leave. Some of us never told a soul.

But the wound remained.

This chapter is divided into two parts—because abuse is not a single story. One speaks to the pain of **abusive relationships**—when love becomes fear, and leaving becomes survival. The other speaks to the ache of **childhood abuse**—when the people who were meant to protect you became the ones who hurt you most.

Both forms of abuse leave echoes. But both also hold the possibility of healing. Of naming what was never yours to carry. Of walking away—not just from a person, but from a lie.

And sometimes, the first step is reading a story that says:

It wasn't your fault.
You were always worthy.
You still are.

Abusive Relationships

Leaving to Live

Some stories are not whispered—they are held in silence so deep, it becomes a second skin. For many women, abuse is not a single moment of violence but a long, slow erosion of worth, spirit, and autonomy.

This chapter is written for those women. The ones who stayed too long because they were afraid. The ones who left and still wonder if they were right to do so. The ones who knew they deserved better but didn't know how to begin again.

It is also for my mother. She stayed for the same reason many women do: survival. With four children and no income, she bore the weight of someone else's rage so her daughters could eat, sleep, and grow. She taught me that love and sacrifice are not always opposites—but I also came to understand that staying is not always a failure of courage. Sometimes, it's simply the only path that seems open at the time.

This chapter is also for two women I deeply care about. They each lived through years of emotional abuse, their spirits slowly dimming beneath the weight of false hope. They stayed longer than they should have—because they loved deeply, believed in change, and hoped that kindness could mend what pain had worn down. But in time, they found the courage to walk away.

And today, they are building new, joy-filled lives—without their abusers, without apology, and without regret.

For every woman who has endured harm disguised as love, I offer this truth: healing begins not when the abuser apologizes (most never do), but when you decide you are worthy of safety, dignity, and joy.

You are the heroine of this story—and it's not too late to begin again.

Book Friends
Girl A: A Novel by Abigail Dean
A survivor of a cult-like abusive household, the protagonist navigates the scars left behind and the media attention surrounding her escape. Told with haunting restraint, this is a story about memory, control, and reclaiming the right to one's own truth.

> *Why it helps:* This novel explores the long shadow of emotional and psychological abuse. It offers readers insight into the aftermath of survival—and the quiet courage it takes to speak up after being silenced.

Breath, Eyes, Memory by Edwidge Danticat
A young Haitian girl is sent to New York to reunite with a mother she barely knows. As she uncovers the inherited trauma passed down through generations, she begins the long journey of breaking the cycle.

> *Why it helps:* This story tenderly explores how silence and shame are passed between women—and how they can be healed. It affirms the strength it takes to confront inherited pain and forge a new path.

The Wife by Meg Wolitzer
Joan Castleman has spent forty years subjugating her own literary talent to bolster her husband's career. On the eve of him receiving a major literary award, she finally decides she's done playing the supportive role.

> *Why it helps:* Because it peels back the layers of a long marriage built on silence and sacrifice—and reminds us that it's never too late to rewrite your story.

The Recovery of Rose Gold by **Stephanie Wrobel**
A chilling psychological drama about a young woman raised to believe she was chronically ill—until she discovers her mother's manipulation. Years later, and newly independent, Rose Gold invites her estranged mother back into her life—but not for the reasons she claims.

> *Why it helps:* Because it explores the long reach of maternal control and the quiet, complex journey of reclaiming autonomy after emotional abuse. This novel validates the slow, often messy process of waking up to betrayal—and finding one's voice on the other side.

Black and Blue by **Anna Quindlen**
After years of abuse, Fran leaves her husband and starts a new life with her young son under an assumed identity. But fear and memory follow her, even in freedom.

> *Why it helps:* This novel doesn't glamorize survival—it shows the ongoing emotional cost of leaving.

She Walked

She walked—
not because the door was open,
but because her spirit
could no longer fit
inside the shrinking shape
of that life.

She walked without a plan,
with trembling hands,
and a spine stiffened
by every silent night.

She walked not to punish,
but to preserve.
Not to abandon,
but to begin again.

She walked carrying shame
that was never hers,
and stories she was told
not to tell.

She walked because love
shouldn't hurt,
and hope shouldn't hinge
on someone else's healing.

She walked—
into the unknown,
into a life
that finally fit the shape of her soul.

Childhood Abuse

When the Hurt Came Early

Not all abuse leaves bruises. Sometimes, it lives in the silence after a slammed door. In the rules you never dared question. In the fear of being "too loud," "too late," or just "too much."

Some children are hurt not by strangers but by the people meant to protect them. A father's rage. A mother's helplessness. The weight of punishment handed down in the name of love. This section is for those children—now grown—who are still flinching at raised voices, still second-guessing their worth, still carrying the ache of what was never safe to speak. It's for the ones who learned early how to disappear, how to please, and how to survive a house that felt like a storm.

These stories don't retell your childhood—but they may help you understand it. They offer language for what was once endured in silence. They offer mirrors, not for blame but for recognition. Because healing begins when we name what happened and remember that it was never our fault.

Personal Reflection

For much of my life, I saw my father's abuse through the lens of what he did to my mother. Her suffering was visible—acknowledged. Ours wasn't. But we lived under the same fear.

He was rarely physically violent with us, but the threat of it—his temper, his rules, his belt—hung in the air like weather. We didn't speak back. We didn't run late.

We tiptoed. We apologized for things that weren't our fault. We mistook obedience for safety. It took me years to come to terms with the truth: we were abused, too. Not in the ways people talk about in books or on the news, but in the slow, suffocating way in which control seeps into a house and teaches children to be afraid of being themselves.

I say this now for every woman who thought her father's violence "wasn't that bad," or who told herself, "he only hit me once" or "he never touched me." If you were made small, afraid, voiceless—*you were hurt.*

And it matters.

This chapter is for us. The daughters who feared the adult who made the rules. The ones who became peacekeepers, perfectionists, or protectors. The ones who didn't realize, until much later, that surviving something doesn't mean it didn't hurt.

Book Friends

These novels explore the emotional and psychological impact of childhood abuse, neglect, and control—and the long road to self-understanding and healing. Each story reveals a different way in which a child can be wounded—and how adults can carry that pain until it is named, felt, and released.

White Oleander by Janet Fitch

Astrid is passed from foster home to foster home after her mother, a glamorous but poisonous poet, is imprisoned for murder. Each chapter of her adolescence unfolds through abandonment, betrayal, and the desperate search for identity in the absence of real love.

> ***Why it helps:*** Because it gives voice to the invisible wounds left by emotionally manipulative parents. This novel explores how children internalize pain—and how, even in the aftermath of betrayal, it's possible to reclaim a sense of self, truth, and beauty.

The Ocean at the End of the Lane by Neil Gaiman

A man returns to his childhood home and is flooded by memories of a terrifying and magical time in his youth—one marked by fear, manipulation, and abandonment.

Why it helps: This haunting novel captures the blurred line between childhood fear and fantasy.

Bastard Out of Carolina by Dorothy Allison

Bone, a young girl growing up poor in the American South, endures physical and sexual abuse from her stepfather.

Why it helps: This raw, unflinching book offers one of the most powerful portrayals of childhood abuse in fiction.

Room by Emma Donoghue

Told from the perspective of five-year-old Jack, who has spent his entire life in captivity with his mother, this novel explores trauma, escape, and the difficulty of reintegrating into the outside world

Why it helps: By allowing us to see trauma through a child's innocent lens, this book offers a profound look at attachment, survival, and the fierce love between a mother and her son.

Addiction, Recovery & Return

When the Thread Breaks

For a time, I worked with two young adults navigating the depths of addiction. They weren't just clients. They became like my own. And that, in the end, is why I had to stop.

The boundaries blurred—not because I didn't know better, but because the heart doesn't always listen to training. When someone calls at 11:00 p.m., begging to sleep on your floor so they don't end up in a bar—and you know they're a good kid, not just a client—how do you say no?

It changed me. Deepened me. But it also stretched me beyond my limits. I realized that the cost of caring that much was not something I could sustain.

Addiction can be easy to judge from the outside. Until you've lived inside it—your own, or someone else's—you may not realize how quiet it can be, how easily it begins, or how long it hides.

It doesn't always look like rock bottom. Sometimes, it looks like functioning. Like showing up. Like holding everything together while falling apart inside. It can wear the face of ambition or motherhood, the disguise of social drinking, or or the silence of emotional chronic pain.

Addiction is often less about the substance than the ache beneath it. It's about trying to numb something, escape something, or fill a space that once held connection, safety, or love.

And yet, it's not a moral failing. It's a longing—for relief, for rest, for permission to not hurt.

Book Friends

The stories in this section are not cautionary tales. They are quiet invitations—to witness, to understand, to remember that healing is rarely linear and never simple. Some of these characters relapse. Some resist help. Some recover. Some don't. But each one brings us closer to the truth: that to love someone who has an addiction, or to be someone in recovery, is to live with vulnerability, with courage, and with the ever-present possibility of return.

If you are holding this story—your own, or someone else's—these pages are for you. Not to solve the pain, but to soften the shame. To remind you that healing is not about perfection. It's about re-choosing yourself, even on the days you feel lost.

These are stories of unraveling—and of coming back home.

Shuggie Bain by Douglas Stuart

A searing, beautiful novel about a young boy growing up in 1980s Glasgow with an alcoholic mother. Equal parts heartbreak and devotion, it reveals the toll addiction takes on families—and the resilience that survives it.

> *Why it helps:* Because it shows how addiction doesn't just shape the addict; it reshapes every room, every relationship, every silence in a household.

We Are the Light by Matthew Quick

A quiet and redemptive story about trauma, therapy, and the community that forms around one man's healing.

> *Why it helps:* Because it reminds us that healing doesn't always come from within—it often comes from being seen, held, and mirrored by others.

The Summer of Bitter and Sweet by Jen Ferguson

Set in the Canadian prairies, this novel explores intergenerational trauma, sexual violence, and the pull toward addictive patterns.

Why it helps: Because it shows how pain can echo across generations—but so can courage. This story helps name the shadows while honoring the strength it takes to step into the light.

Stay With Me by Sandra Rodriguez Barron

A lyrical and quietly devastating novel about a young woman grappling with memory, trauma, and addiction as she returns to the island where a pivotal childhood moment shaped her life. As she reconnects with others who share her past, the story unfolds with deep tenderness and emotional realism.

Why it helps: Because it shows how addiction often masks deeper grief. This novel doesn't sensationalize recovery; it treats it as a process of returning to the parts of ourselves that were lost too early and finding connection through shared pain.

Recovery Road by Blake Nelson

A raw but redemptive story of a teenage girl's journey through rehab and the complicated path of returning to real life. Grounded, relatable, and emotionally clear.

Why it helps: Because it honors the nonlinear truth of recovery. This story offers hope without illusion and shows how healing often begins in the messiest, most honest moments.

What Addiction Tries to Tell Us

And what story gently reminds us instead

Addiction is not always about the substance. It's about what we've been taught to silence, numb, or carry alone.

It tries to tell us:
- You are too much.
- You are not enough.
- You need this to survive.
- You don't deserve better.
- You're the only one.

But story reminds us:
- You are not alone.
- You are not broken.
- You are loved—even in your lowest moment.
- You can begin again.
- There is no shame in asking for help.

Addiction isolates.

Fiction reconnects.

Sometimes, reading a story where someone else survives the spiral is the first step toward believing you might, too.

Recovering from Trauma

Living with the Echo

Trauma reshapes us. It changes how we see the world. How we trust. How we speak to ourselves in the dark. Whether it stems from loss, violence, betrayal, or the slow erosion of safety, trauma leaves behind more than pain. It leaves questions, patterns, silence. And for many of us, it leaves a long, invisible story that we're still trying to tell.

And yet—trauma does not define us. It challenges us, yes. But it also offers the possibility of transformation. Healing from trauma is not linear. It does not happen all at once. It arrives in fragments:

- *A deeper breath*
- *A new boundary*
- *A moment when something once terrifying feels...less so.*

For some, healing begins in stillness. For others, it begins in story. Fiction offers a sacred space to explore trauma safely. It lets us witness what we've felt but never spoken. Through characters who carry what we carry, we begin to understand our own pain with greater tenderness. We see survival. We see transformation. And, crucially, we see that we are not alone. These stories don't erase what happened. They don't pretend everything can be fixed. But they sit beside us—gently—until we remember that we are more than what we endured.

Book Friends

The books in this section illuminate different paths through trauma:

Reclaiming identity after loss

Trusting again after betrayal

Naming long-held grief

Finding moments of grace in the aftermath of fear

These novels hold both ache and hope, reminding us that while trauma may leave its mark, it does not write our ending.

Tell the Wolves I'm Home by Carol Rifka Brunt

Fourteen-year-old June Elbus is reeling after the death of her beloved uncle Finn, a famous painter who succumbs to AIDS during the height of the epidemic. When she meets Toby, Finn's grieving partner, the unlikely friendship that blossoms helps June unravel the complex web of secrecy, shame, and sorrow that surrounds her family—and herself.

> *Why it helps:* Because it explores grief, misunderstood love, and the wounds we carry when truth is withheld.

The Kite Runner by Khaled Hosseini

A young boy named Amir betrays his childhood friend Hassan, and that betrayal shapes the rest of his life. Years later, Amir returns to Afghanistan to confront what he ran from and find a path toward redemption.

> *Why it helps:* This novel gently explores shame, guilt, and the long-lasting effects of emotional trauma. It reminds us that healing often begins with truth—and that forgiveness, of self and others, is part of that path.

The Great Alone by Kristin Hannah

Leni's family moves to the remote wilderness of Alaska, where her father, a Vietnam War veteran, battles PTSD. Isolated and unstable, the family unravels in the shadow of his trauma

Why it helps: A powerful story of survival, this novel explores intergenerational trauma and the quiet strength required to break cycles. It shows us that even in the darkest winters, there is the possibility of spring.

The Shadow of the Wind by **Carlos Ruiz Zafón**
In post-WWII Barcelona, young Daniel is drawn into the mystery of a forgotten author, uncovering buried secrets and hidden traumas as he pieces together the past.

Why it helps: This atmospheric story speaks to the power of confronting what has long been hidden. It reminds us that healing often requires excavation—and courage.

The Goldfinch by **Donna Tartt**
Theo survives a terrorist attack that kills his mother. He clings to a stolen painting as his life spirals through grief, guilt, and isolation.

Why it helps: A masterful exploration of the way trauma shapes identity. It affirms that healing is rarely linear but still possible, even when it feels messy and slow.

Small Great Things by **Jodi Picoult**
When Ruth, an African American nurse, is ordered not to touch a white supremacist's newborn, tragedy unfolds—and Ruth must navigate the trauma of racism, injustice, and survival.

Why it helps: This book addresses the trauma imposed by systemic racism. It offers readers the chance to witness internal transformation and the deep need for empathy in any healing journey.

The Myth of Normal: Trauma, Illness, and Healing in a Toxic Culture by Dr. Gabor Maté *(nonfiction)*

In this wide-ranging and insightful book, Dr. Maté explores how trauma—both personal and societal—manifests in the body, mind, and culture. Drawing from decades of clinical practice, he challenges the idea that illness is separate from life experience and shows how healing is possible when we address root causes, not just symptoms.

> *Why it helps:* Because it reframes trauma not as a flaw, but as an adaptive response to suffering. Maté's wisdom invites us to befriend our wounds, understand their origins, and begin to live from a place of wholeness rather than survival.

When Things Fall Apart: Heart Advice for Difficult Times by Pema Chödrön *(nonfiction)*

A beloved spiritual guide, Pema Chödrön offers gentle, grounded wisdom for moments when life feels unmanageable. Drawing from Tibetan Buddhist teachings, she invites readers to lean into pain rather than resist it—to soften in the face of fear, uncertainty, and grief, and to discover peace in the very heart of chaos.

> *Why it helps:* Because it teaches that falling apart is not the end—but a beginning. This book is a compassionate companion for anyone navigating deep loss, anxiety, or change, reminding us that healing arises not from avoiding pain, but from staying present with it.

The House of the Soul

(inspired by Khalil Gibran)

The house of the soul has many rooms.
Some lit by joy, some dimmed by grief,
and others still waiting
to be entered without fear.

Do not rush past the sorrowing rooms—
they are not empty.
They hold the relics of who you've been,
and the seeds of who you are becoming.

Open each door gently.
Sit for a while.
Even in the quietest chambers,
love has left a light on.

Grief & Loss

Grief, The Quiet Companion

Grief is not a single moment. It is not just the funeral. Or the diagnosis. Or the last goodbye.

Grief is what happens after. After the casseroles stop coming. After the inbox fills but your arms remain empty. After the world keeps moving—and you're not sure how to follow. It arrives like a thunderclap and stays like fog. Sometimes sharp. Sometimes silent. But always near.

Grief doesn't keep a calendar. It doesn't care about closure. It arrives on its own terms—and often stays longer than we're allowed to admit. It circles back unexpectedly—with a scent, a song, a chair that no one else sits in anymore.

We grieve people, yes. But also roles we've lost. Versions of ourselves we'll never be again. Places that once felt like home. Relationships that didn't end in death but dissolved all the same.

We grieve what never happened, what happened too soon, what changed without our permission. And the hardest part? We are often expected to carry it privately. To show up smiling, productive, composed, while the landscape of our life has been split in two.

This section is not about moving on. It is about moving *with*. Letting grief walk beside us like a quiet companion—not always visible, but always felt. Because grief, at its core, is love with nowhere to go. And stories can offer it shelter—not to fix the pain, but to hold it. Name it. Soften it. And remind us that we are not the only ones who have ever wept in public, or in secret, or in the middle of a beautiful moment we couldn't share with the one we still miss.

The books in this section do not offer escape. They offer presence. They sit with us when we cannot explain ourselves.

They honor the depth of what was lost—and the courage it takes to stay open to life anyway.

This is grief, not as an enemy to overcome but as a companion to walk with as we find our way forward, carrying love that never left.

Book Friends

These books don't ask us to "get over it." They sit beside us in the ache, offering language, presence, and quiet companionship as we learn to carry what cannot be changed.

Lincoln in the Bardo by George Saunders

An imaginative, moving novel set in the space between life and death. Based on Abraham Lincoln's grief for his son, it offers a profound meditation on mourning, liminality, and love that lingers.

> *Why it helps:* This novel creates a sacred space between worlds—between holding on and letting go. It reminds us that grief reshapes time, and that love, once given, doesn't vanish with the body.

The Friend by Sigrid Nunez

After a friend's death, a woman inherits his dog and unexpectedly begins to process her sorrow. Quiet, philosophical, and gently humorous—a meditation on grief, writing, and unexpected companionship.

> *Why it helps:* Grief is rarely neat—and this story honors its messiness with grace. It shows how companionship (even from a dog) and creative expression can carry us when words fall short.

The Lovely Bones by Alice Sebold

Told from the perspective of a murdered teenage girl watching her family grieve, this novel is both tragic and redemptive. It explores loss from both sides of the veil.

> *Why it helps:* This book validates the lingering presence of those we've lost. It comforts those who wonder where their loved ones have gone—and whether they're still near.

The Year of Magical Thinking by Joan Didion *(nonfiction)*

A luminous memoir written in the raw aftermath of Joan Didion's husband's sudden death. With unflinching clarity, she captures the altered mental state of grief—what she calls "magical thinking"—where logic and longing intertwine, and time loses meaning.

> *Why it helps:* Because it doesn't ask you to move on. It simply bears witness to the disorientation that follows great loss—the belief that things might return, that the door might open, that this can't be final. This book offers no cliché or comfort. Just presence. Precision. And the quiet companionship of someone who has lived inside the fog and found words for it.

The Beauty of What Remains by Steve Leder *(nonfiction)*

Written by a rabbi who has sat beside thousands of grieving families, this book offers quiet wisdom drawn from the threshold between life and death. With compassion and clarity, Leder reflects on what truly matters when everything else falls away.

Why it helps: Because it meets grief with softness—not answers. This book doesn't preach or push. It simply invites reflection. For those carrying long, quiet sorrow, it offers gentle companionship. And for those who may not say they're grieving—but feel it in their bones—it provides a safe, sacred space to begin naming what remains.

Closing Reflection: Carrying the Quiet

Grief changes form, but it doesn't disappear. It becomes part of the way we listen. The way we pause at certain songs. The way we hold joy more tenderly, knowing how easily it can vanish.

If you are still carrying sorrow—visible or hidden—let this be your reminder: You are not behind. You are not doing it wrong. You are living with love that had nowhere else to go.

There is no need to rush toward resolution. No gold star for how "well" you've healed. The measure is in your gentleness. Your continued openness. Your willingness to feel—despite the cost.

Some days, the ache will rise like a tide. Let it. Other days, it will lie still like a stone in your pocket. You do not have to explain either.

You are allowed to laugh. You are allowed to cry. You are allowed to hold both in the same breath. If all you've done today is keep going—you've done enough. This is not the end of grief. But it may be the beginning of learning how to live *beside* it, not *beneath* it.

She Carries It

She doesn't talk about it
much anymore.
The world moved on,
and so—
she learned to nod.
To smile.
To ask about the weather
instead of the ache.

But the grief is still there.
It rides in the car with her.
It shops for groceries.
It sits quietly
in the passenger seat
when she hears
that one song
and doesn't cry—
but almost does.

It's not sharp like
it was.
It's softer now.
Like sea glass.
Rounded by time,
but still part of her.

Some days, it rises.
At a scent.
A season.
The way someone laughs
just like him.
The way no one calls
on the day

she always remembers.

She doesn't need pity.
She doesn't need fixing.
She needs space—
to still miss him,
to still feel it,
to carry love
without apology.

Because grief doesn't vanish—
it weaves itself in.
But so does joy.
Quietly, at first.
Then in full colour.

One morning,
she laughs without guilt.
One afternoon,
she dances in the kitchen.
One evening,
she looks at the sky—
and feels more wonder
than weight.

This too is love.
To keep living.
To let the light back in.
To carry both sorrow and joy—
and know there is room
for all of it.

Forgiveness (Self & Others)

Not For Them—For You

Forgiveness is not a door we walk through. It's a thread we pick up—sometimes shakily, sometimes with resistance—and begin to weave through the frayed fabric of our hearts. It doesn't arrive with clarity or finality. More often, it arrives after grief. After fury. After long silences and even longer internal battles.

This section isn't about easy absolutions. It's about the kind of forgiveness that's earned slowly, quietly—if at all. The kind that begins not with a grand act but with a small decision: *I don't want this pain to live inside me forever.*

Forgiveness is often misunderstood—

As permission.
As forgetting.
As reconciliation.

But true forgiveness—especially for women who have carried betrayal, neglect, abuse, or abandonment—is not about the other person. It's about release. It's about reclaiming your emotional real estate.

It's saying: *"This is mine now. Not yours. And I'm choosing peace—not because you deserve it, but because I do."*

To forgive does not mean we deny the harm. It means we stop letting it shape our worth. It means we make peace with the truth so we can walk forward without dragging the weight of someone else's actions behind us.

And yet, there is no timeline. No right way. Some days, we feel whole again. Other days, the wound reopens with a smell, a song, a memory. Forgiveness is not a straight line; it's a spiral. We return to it, again and again, each time with a little more compassion for ourselves.

Sometimes, the person we need to forgive is not a parent, sibling, ex-lover, or friend. Sometimes, it's ourselves. For the things we didn't know. For the ways we stayed too long. For the harsh inner voices we believed. For not being perfect when all we ever needed to be was real.

Forgiveness is not weak—

> It is wild.
> It is holy.
> It is the moment we say: *"You no longer get to live rent-free in my body, my mind, or my spirit."*

And then—we begin again.

Book Friends

These stories explore forgiveness not as a simple act but as a layered, deeply human process. Whether it's forgiving someone else, forgiving oneself, or learning to live with what cannot be undone, each novel holds space for pain—and the possibility of peace.

The Story of Arthur Truluv by Elizabeth Berg

A gentle novel about an elderly man who finds unexpected friendship with a grieving teenager. As their lives intertwine, both must confront past wounds and regrets. Forgiveness here arrives in everyday acts of kindness and intergenerational love.

> ***Why it helps:*** This story affirms that healing doesn't always come from confrontation but from compassion. It reminds us that forgiveness can grow in unlikely places—through friendship, presence, and grace.

The Last Romantics by Tara Conklin

Spanning nearly a century, this novel tells the story of four siblings bound by love, loss, and a shared childhood trauma.

As they each seek connection, fulfillment, and meaning, the past resurfaces in unexpected ways, forcing them to reckon with old wounds, long-held secrets, and the ways in which they've hurt each other.

> *Why it helps:* Because it captures the complexity of familial forgiveness. It reminds us that love doesn't erase pain—but it can soften it. And that forgiving ourselves and those we love may be the most profound act of healing.

The Orphan's Tale by Pam Jenoff

Set during World War II, this novel tells the story of two women: a Jewish circus performer in hiding and the star aerialist who protects her. Both women carry heavy secrets and betrayals. Their journey is one of sacrifice, loss, and eventual forgiveness in the face of haunting choices.

> *Why it helps:* This novel explores how forgiveness can be forged not in comfort but in survival. It shows that even in the most impossible circumstances, grace is still possible—both between women and within ourselves.

The Midnight Library by Matt Haig

Between life and death, there is a library—and within it, an endless array of lives one could have lived. Nora Seed enters this space in a moment of despair, believing she's failed everyone—including herself. But as she explores the many versions of her life, she slowly begins to see her choices, regrets, and worth through new eyes.

Why it helps: This novel gently affirms that self-forgiveness is often about perspective. It reminds us that even the smallest choices carry meaning—and that being human means we will falter, question, and still be worthy of grace.

The Language of Flowers by Vanessa Diffenbaugh

After aging out of the foster system, Victoria Jones finds herself alone, angry, and unsure how to love—or be loved. But through the Victorian meanings of flowers, she begins to express what she cannot yet say aloud. As she builds a new life, she must reckon with a traumatic past and learn how to forgive herself for the choices she made in survival.

Why it helps: This story holds space for self-forgiveness as a tender, nonlinear process. It speaks to the healing power of expression and reminds us that rebuilding a life—however slowly—is its own kind of redemption.

The Deepest Secret by Carla Buckley

A mother keeps a devastating secret to protect her son, who has a rare medical condition that makes sunlight deadly. But when tragedy strikes and the truth begins to surface, every relationship in their tightly wound community is tested.

Why it helps: Because it explores the blurry lines between right and wrong, and the heavy cost of choices made in love. This novel offers a compelling portrait of self-forgiveness and the complex grace required to let go of guilt when no one else can.

Left to Tell **by Immaculée Ilibagiza** *(nonfiction)*
A profound memoir of surviving the Rwandan genocide, written with raw grace and spiritual clarity. Immaculée's ability to forgive the men who murdered her family is not just remarkable—it is radical.

> ***Why it helps:*** This memoir is a sacred reminder that forgiveness is a soul decision. It shows how spiritual depth, inner strength, and grace can lead us beyond unimaginable loss and into light.

Forgiveness ≠ Reconciliation

There's a quiet misconception that forgiveness must lead to reconciliation. But the two are not the same.

Forgiveness is an internal act. It is the choice to release resentment and reclaim your emotional energy. It happens within you, for you—even if the person who harmed you never changes, never apologizes, or never returns.

Reconciliation, on the other hand, is relational. It requires mutual accountability. It depends on trust being rebuilt, safety being re-established, and a new chapter being co-created by both people involved.

You can forgive someone and never speak to them again. You can forgive and still hold boundaries. You can forgive without forgetting—because remembering is part of healing.

Forgiveness is not about excusing harm. It's about refusing to carry it. And sometimes, the most radical form of self-love is saying:

I release you. But I do not return to you.

The Shape of Forgiveness

It doesn't arrive all at once—
not as lightning,
not as light.
Forgiveness is slower than that.
Quieter.

It comes in pieces—
a softened memory,
a breath that no longer catches,
a day you stop rehearsing the wound.

You think you'll feel ready.
But mostly, you just grow tired
of holding the weight.

So you begin.
Not because they asked.
Not because they changed.
But because *you* deserve to move freely
through the chambers of your own heart.

Forgiveness is not forgetting.
It is remembering with less ache.
It is no longer letting their shadow
darken your joy.

It is reclaiming your peace
without needing them to see it.
It is choosing—again and again—
to unhook your worth
from their harm.

Section 2: Inner Struggles & Self-Perception

We are born with the ache to belong. To be seen. To be known. To find a place where we don't have to explain or shrink or hide what hurts.

But life doesn't always grant us that ease. Sometimes, we are strangers in our own families. Sometimes, the world tells us we don't fit the mold—and then asks us to thank it for letting us stay.

This section is for anyone who has ever stood at the edge of belonging. For those who have felt the silence of a room that should have welcomed them. Or the absence of a love that should have stayed.

These stories offer more than connection. They offer *recognition*. Not just of who you are—but of all the places you've searched for home.

Let these pages remind you: belonging is not something you earn. It's something you reclaim.

And it starts with being true to yourself even when no one else is watching.

Body Image

What the Mirror Misses

Body image is not a vanity issue. It is an identity issue. A cultural issue. A spiritual issue. And for women, it is almost always a wound.

It begins early—sometimes before we even know we're being watched. A comment at a family dinner. A magazine left open on a coffee table. A mother skipping meals. A father pointing at a stranger and saying, "She's really let herself go." And suddenly, we are learning not only what bodies look like—but which ones are allowed to be loved.

From then on, the body becomes a project. Something to fix. To manage. To discipline. Praise becomes currency, and weight becomes a verdict. Some of us shrink ourselves in the hope of being accepted. Others rebel against the system—only to carry shame anyway.

And here's the tragedy: It doesn't end when we grow up. For many women, the pressure intensifies. We are expected to age without aging. To be confident without being "too much." To be soft without softness. Strong without taking up space. And always—always—grateful.

But this section isn't about blame. It's about truth. It's about naming the inherited pain, the unspoken hunger, and the private mirrors we no longer want to fear. This section is for: The woman who has been praised for her beauty but never felt beautiful; the woman who avoids photos, not out of vanity but out of shame; the woman whose weight has changed, and with it, her place in the world; the woman who's tired of starving—for food, for affirmation, for freedom.

Your body is not the enemy. And beauty is not a performance. You were never too much. Or not enough. You were always becoming.

Let these stories reflect you back to yourself—not the curated version, but the true one. The one who still remembers joy in movement. Laughter without shrinking. Sensuality without shame.

Welcome back to your body. It missed you.

Book Friends
Stories that reclaim the body from shame, silence, and societal judgment

These stories hold more than characters—they hold mirrors. Each one explores a woman's relationship with her body, her reflection, her hunger, and the stories she's been told about what makes her enough. Some are fierce. Some are tender. All of them dare to name what the mirror often misses: that beauty is not compliance—it's reclamation.

13 Ways of Looking at a Fat Girl by Mona Awad
This novel follows Lizzie, a young woman who sees her body as a battleground. As she loses weight, she finds herself no closer to happiness—only deeper in self-judgment.

> ***Why it helps:*** Because it names the quiet war many women fight with their own reflection—and shows that losing weight doesn't always lighten the emotional load.

Dietland by Sarai Walker
Plum is waiting to lose weight so she can finally live. Then a radical feminist group intervenes—and her life explodes into purpose, power, and fury.

> ***Why it helps:*** Because it dismantles the fantasy of "thin equals happy" and replaces it with something far more liberating: radical self-possession.

Big Girl by Mecca Jamilah Sullivan
Malaya navigates childhood in Harlem through the lens of fatness, food, and silence. Lush, tender, and cutting.

> *Why it helps:* Because it tells the truth about what it means to grow up in a body others see before they see you–and it doesn't flinch.

The List by Siobhan Vivian
Each year, a high school ranks two girls from every grade as "prettiest" and "ugliest." What unfolds is a brutal dissection of appearance and hierarchy.

> *Why it helps:* Because it mirrors how early and how deeply we internalize beauty standards–and the emotional fallout of public judgment.

Body Positive Power by Megan Jayne Crabbe *(nonfiction)*
Part memoir, part manifesto, this book dismantles diet culture with fierce honesty and radical joy. Crabbe offers tools and truths to help readers stop fighting their bodies and start living in them.

> *Why it helps:* Because it dismantles the lies we've been sold about our bodies and offers radical, joyful permission to live fully in them.

She Stopped Apologizing to the Mirror

She used to stand in front of the mirror
like it was a courtroom.
Every line, every curve,
another piece of evidence against her.

She learned early how to smile without joy,
how to shrink her hunger,
how to praise other women
while secretly punishing herself.

She thought confidence meant achievement.
That softness was weakness. That beauty had a size.
That being seen required permission.

But one day—
not dramatic, not loud—
she looked in the mirror,
and instead of adjusting, fixing, judging…
she stayed.

She breathed. And said the only words that mattered:
"You are okay.
You are beautiful.
I love you."

No conditions.
And for the first time,
the mirror wasn't the one watching.
She was.

Self-Worth & Identity

She Forgot She Was Enough

There are many ways to lose yourself. Not all of them look like crisis. Some look like achievement. Some look like being the dependable one. The thin one. The nice one. The high performer. The one who doesn't ask for much.

Sometimes, we become so good at being who the world wants us to be, we forget who we were before we began editing ourselves.

This section is for the woman who doubts her worth unless it's proven. Unless someone says she's enough. Unless she's accomplished something, fixed something, pleased someone.

It's for the one who still hears the voice from childhood: *"Who do you think you are?"* And the one who learned to answer it with apology.

It's for the woman who looks in the mirror and sees not her essence, but her performance. Her mistakes. Her age. Her softness where there used to be sharpness.

And it's also for the one who's beginning to wake up—who's quietly, tentatively asking: *What if I was never broken? What if I don't need to earn love anymore?*

Because self-worth isn't something we hustle for. It's something we come home to. It's not built through perfection. It's revealed through presence. Through shedding what was never really ours: the shame, the pressure, the mask.

Fiction helps us remember who we are behind the performance. It gives us characters who fail, who fall, who hide—and who, eventually, find their way back. Not because someone finally validates them, but because they finally learn to *see themselves*.

This section is your invitation to do the same.

Book Friends

Self-worth isn't something we achieve. It's something we remember—after years of forgetting. These stories hold women who've twisted themselves into shapes to be loved, accepted, or praised... and who, in their own time, begin to say: *"Enough."*

Each book reflects a different path home—some quiet, some fierce, all true. They are companions for the woman remembering she was never broken—just buried.

The Vanishing Half by Brit Bennett

In a world that rewards erasure, two sisters live opposing lives—one rooted, one passing. Their choices ripple across generations, shaping daughters, identities, and the meaning of home.

> *Why it helps:* Because it explores the emotional cost of becoming someone you're not—and the strength in reclaiming who you are. It's a poignant reminder that wholeness begins where hiding ends.

The Awakening by Kate Chopin

A woman begins to sense the shape of her own desires and voice beyond the roles imposed on her. As the tide of expectation pulls against her, she begins to choose herself—for the first time.

> *Why it helps:* Because it speaks the truth that freedom isn't selfish—it's essential to becoming whole. It reminds us that awakening is often quiet, personal, and powerfully irreversible.

Fates and Furies by Lauren Groff

Told from two perspectives within a long marriage, this richly layered novel reveals hidden dimensions of love, art, and identity.

> *Why it helps:* Because it exposes how worth can hide behind performance—and the quiet liberation of stepping out from behind the curtain.

The Book of Form and Emptiness by Ruth Ozeki

After the death of his father, a young boy begins to hear the voices of inanimate objects, while his mother descends into emotional chaos. What unfolds is a luminous, layered story about grief, identity, and the stories we carry.

> *Why it helps:* Because it shows how worth can be reclaimed not through silence or fixing, but by listening to the quiet truths we've long ignored—including our own.

My Name Is Lucy Barton by Elizabeth Strout

In a hospital room, suspended between illness and healing, Lucy begins a halting, tender conversation with her estranged mother—unearthing a lifetime of hidden pain, self-doubt, and longing for belonging.

> *Why it helps:* Because it reflects how self-worth can be shaped by what's unsaid—and how, even without full reconciliation, we can begin to write ourselves anew.

The Cost of Disappearing

From an early age, many women are taught to seek approval instead of alignment. Be nice. Be small. Don't ask for too much Don't make people uncomfortable. Don't be too loud, too smart, too ambitious, too emotional, too anything.

This conditioning doesn't just limit us—it *splinters* us. It teaches us to edit ourselves for belonging. To trade authenticity for acceptance. To measure worth by productivity, thinness, approval, or sacrifice. And over time, this becomes so familiar, it feels like identity. But it's not. It's adaptation.

Real identity often waits beneath the layers we've shed to survive. And recovering it means unlearning what was rewarded—and remembering what was real.

This section is a small step in that direction. Toward wholeness. Toward truth. Toward the quiet, radical act of saying: *"I was always enough. I just forgot."*

She Forgot She Was Enough

She forgot she was enough. Not all at once.
It happened in the quiet spaces—
where praise spoke louder than presence,
and being helpful felt safer than being whole.

She learned to smile when her heart whispered, *No*.
She waited for someone else
to name her worth.

She became who they needed—
sharp in rooms that valued brilliance,
soft in rooms that punished it.
Competent to the point of depletion,
wearing exhaustion like a badge.

But beneath it all,
there was always something else.
A quieter self—
unimpressed by applause,
uninterested in perfection.

The self that remembered joy without permission
The self that didn't shrink, prove, or disappear.

And one day, after all the effort,
after all the shape-shifting,
she looked in the mirror and saw her.

Enough. Still. And always.

Imposter Syndrome

Who Do You Think You Are?

It's the voice that whispers, *You're not really good enough*—even after the book is written, the degree is earned, the room is entered. It's the sensation of walking into a space you've earned, only to feel like you're trespassing. It's the fear that at any moment, someone will discover you're not who they thought you were.

This is imposter syndrome.

It doesn't matter how accomplished, qualified, or gifted you are. Imposter syndrome doesn't feed on facts—it feeds on fear. Fear of being too visible. Fear of being seen and still not being enough. And for women, it often arrives wearing different disguises—

- The need to overprepare before speaking.
- The urge to apologize before offering an idea.
- The belief that success must always be explained, never simply claimed.

We question our belonging not because we are unqualified, but because we have been conditioned to doubt the very idea of *enoughness*. Especially in cultures that reward silence over self-trust.

Many of us were raised to be agreeable, not authoritative. To be pleasant, not powerful. To work twice as hard for half the recognition—and to do so quietly, without needing credit. And so, even when we do succeed, the feeling is fragile. We wonder if it was luck, timing, a generous mentor—anything but our own merit. We assume our confidence is suspicious. Our clarity, threatening. Our presence, conditional.

This is not a personal flaw. It is cultural gaslighting. Because for many women, imposter syndrome isn't about internal insecurity—it's about external messaging. The world still treats confidence in women differently than it does in men. Where men are seen as bold, women are seen as arrogant. Where men are decisive, women are difficult. Where men are seen as leaders, women are seen as exceptions—if they're seen at all.

So, we internalize the fear that we must earn every inch of space, constantly. We become chronic self-editors. We believe that if we're not perfect, we're frauds. That if we falter once, we've been "found out."

But what if imposter syndrome is not a signal that you're unworthy—but a sign that you're stepping into something your lineage wasn't allowed to claim? What if the discomfort isn't proof you don't belong—but proof that you're the first to walk through that particular door? What helps?

Naming it. Imposter syndrome thrives in silence. The moment we say it aloud, we reduce its power.

Normalizing it. Even women at the top of their fields—doctors, CEOs, best-selling authors—speak of this doubt. It's not a flaw in you. It's a feature of the system.

Noticing it—but not obeying it. You can hear the voice and still take the stage. Still send the email. Still share the idea.

Reclaiming your story. You didn't get here by accident. You got here by rising—again and again, often through terrain no one else could see.

You are not a fraud. You are a force that hasn't been fully mirrored yet. And you don't need permission to belong to your own life. Let this be your reminder: You are allowed to take up space. You are allowed to be seen. You are allowed to succeed—without apology, without preamble, and without waiting for someone else to validate your voice. You don't need to prove your worth. You only need to stand in it.

Book Friends

These books don't just depict characters struggling with imposter syndrome; they offer mirrors, metaphors, and moments of reckoning. Some explore the emotional terrain directly, while others offer powerful allegories.

The Candid Life of Meena Dave by **Namrata Patel**

A woman who has always kept herself small discovers she is the heir to a vibrant community and an unexpected legacy—and must reckon with self-worth, cultural invisibility, and the fear of taking up space.

> ***Why it helps:*** Because it reflects the internal conflict of receiving more than you believe you deserve—and learning to say "yes" to your own becoming.

Such a Fun Age by **Kiley Reid**

Beneath its witty surface lies a sharp commentary on how race, class, and performative "wokeness" affect a young woman's sense of belonging and legitimacy—especially in professional spaces.

> ***Why it helps:*** Because it shows how imposter syndrome is not just personal but systemic. A smart, layered reminder of how social forces shape self-perception.

The Bookish Life of Nina Hill by **Abbi Waxman**

A charming novel about an introverted woman who doubts her ability to handle the unpredictability of life—until unexpected connections help her reclaim her place in it.

> ***Why it helps:*** Because it affirms that quiet women are powerful too—and that self-trust doesn't always arrive loudly.

Girl, Woman, Other by **Bernardine Evaristo**
A kaleidoscopic novel offering multiple vignettes of women navigating identity, ambition, and the inner voices that question their right to shine.

> *Why it helps:* Because it captures the many forms imposter syndrome can take, and the beauty of claiming space anyway.

The Vanishing Half by **Brit Bennett**
Explores identity and the roles women perform to fit in, highlighting the cost of hiding and the courage required to reclaim one's truth.

> *Why it helps:* Because it's a haunting, honest look at the masks we wear—and the freedom of letting them go.

The Echo Wife by **Sarah Gailey**
A speculative, emotionally intelligent thriller exploring identity, autonomy, and the versions of ourselves we reject.

> *Why it helps:* Because it's a bold, metaphoric mirror of imposter syndrome and what happens when we split ourselves to survive.

The Other Black Girl by **Zakiya Dalila Harris**
When Nella, the only Black woman at a New York publishing house, is joined by another Black woman, she expects solidarity—but what unfolds is a layered, suspenseful story about workplace microaggressions, self-doubt, identity politics, and the psychological toll of being "the only one."

Why it helps: Because it brilliantly explores the internal and external pressures that erode self-trust, as well as the haunting question: *Who am I when I no longer perform for approval?*

Big Girl, Small Town by Michelle Gallen

Majella O'Neill is a quirky, overlooked woman working at a chip shop in small-town Northern Ireland. She lives by routine, avoids attention, and has long muted her voice. But as her world subtly shifts, she begins to rediscover her sense of agency and her own quiet strength.

Why it helps: Because it champions the kind of self-trust that builds slowly, beneath the radar. Majella's arc reminds us that being unseen doesn't mean being unworthy—and that quiet resilience is its own form of brilliance.

The Secret Thoughts of Successful Women by Valerie Young *(nonfiction)*

A practical guide that explores why capable, high-achieving women often feel like frauds—and how to break free from the self-sabotaging patterns of imposter syndrome.

Why it helps: Because it names the experience directly and provides grounded, research-backed tools to move through it.

Who Do You Think You Are?

They asked it with a smirk.
With silence.
With raised eyebrows and unreturned emails.
Who do you think you are?

And for a long time, you didn't know
how to answer.

You dimmed. Softened.
Folded your brilliance into smaller shapes.

You apologized for your insight.
Laughed off your longing.

You let them mistake
your humility for doubt.

But the voice never left you.
The one beneath the noise.
The one that
didn't need permission.

And one day, instead of asking,
you remembered.

You are the fire that didn't go out.
The ache that turned to vision.
The silence that became a story.

Mental Wellbeing

When the Mind Grows Heavy: Anxiety & Depression

There is a quiet kind of suffering that can go unseen by the world. It doesn't always announce itself with tears or chaos. Sometimes, it looks like distance. Like pulling away. Like a woman who keeps showing up—at work, at dinner, in conversation—while inside she feels like she's disappearing.

Anxiety and depression are not just diagnoses. They are lived landscapes. They change how the light falls. They dull pleasure. They amplify fear. They whisper things that aren't true—like, *You're alone, You'll never feel better, Something is wrong with you.*

And while the world often encourages resilience, it rarely understands what that actually means in the context of mental struggle. Resilience isn't about pretending to be okay. It's about staying present through pain. About recognizing that even if you're walking through fog, you're still walking. Still alive. Still capable of reaching out, even if your hand trembles when you do.

This chapter is not here to fix that pain, but it is here to speak to it. Because fiction can do something remarkable: It can meet you where you are. It doesn't require explanation or cheerfulness. It doesn't ask you to "snap out of it." It simply offers companionship on the page—through characters who carry shadows too. Through stories that say, *"I've been there. I see you. Keep going."*

These stories don't bypass the dark. They walk with you through it. And that matters. Because sometimes, healing begins not with a solution but with the feeling that you are not alone in what you carry. Not broken. Not invisible.

And that is something the right story can give you—without demand or diagnosis. It can offer rest to the overworked mind.

Permission to feel what you feel. And slowly, gently, it can awaken the part of you that still believes in light.

In a world growing increasingly chaotic, uncertain, and overstimulated, our mental wellbeing is more than a personal matter—it's a cultural one. We are not designed to absorb this much noise, this much speed, this much disconnection. But fiction can offer a counterbalance. A space to slow down. To feel. To recognize ourselves in someone else's arc—and to remember that even the most fragile chapters are not the end of the story.

Let this section be your pause. Let it be a small breath. A hand on your back. A reminder that healing does not always begin with clarity or courage—it begins with presence. And presence is exactly what these stories offer.

Book Friends

Some days, the mind feels too full. Other days, it feels too far away. These stories are companions for both. They don't rush your healing or tell you to be okay—they simply sit with you, like a quiet friend on a cloudy afternoon. Whether through small acts of connection, courageous honesty, or tender friendships, each book offers a soft landing for the overwhelmed spirit and a gentle reminder: *You are not alone in what you feel.*

The Lido by Libby Page

Set in a London neighborhood, this heartwarming story follows an anxious young journalist and an elderly woman campaigning to save a local swimming pool. As their friendship deepens, both women rediscover joy, purpose, and the healing rhythm of community.

> ***Why it helps:*** Because it reminds us that connection can be a lifeline. This novel celebrates small acts of courage, community, and the quiet return to joy.

Everything Here Is Beautiful by Mira T. Lee

This story follows two sisters: one living with mental illness, the other trying to help without losing herself. It's a tender, layered exploration of identity, freedom, responsibility, and the toll mental illness can take on relationships and selfhood alike.

> *Why it helps:* Because it speaks the truth about complexity. This novel holds space for both love and exhaustion, offering compassion to everyone involved.

The Elegance of the Hedgehog by Muriel Barbery

Set in a Parisian apartment building, this quietly philosophical novel follows two unlikely kindred spirits: Renée, a reclusive concierge with a secret passion for literature, and Paloma, a brilliant but disillusioned twelve-year-old plotting her own quiet exit. Their connection disrupts loneliness and opens the door to meaning, beauty, and unexpected friendship.

> *Why it helps:* Because it speaks to the hidden richness inside lives that appear ordinary. It honours the inner world of the anxious, the introverted, and the quietly despairing—and reminds us that even in the depths of solitude, connection and beauty can still find us.

The Weight of Small Things by Sherri Wood Emmons

A quiet, beautifully written novel about a young girl grappling with loss, confusion, and the disorienting nature of grief. This is a book about sorrow that doesn't shout but instead lingers gently, showing how even small moments of connection can be lifelines.

Why it helps: Because it's soft when you need softness. This story gently affirms that your sadness doesn't have to be loud to be real and worthy of care.

Everything Is Beautiful by Eleanor Ray

Amy Ashton's life has been quietly stuck for years. She hoards objects, avoids people, and lives in a carefully controlled world shaped by unresolved trauma. But when curious new neighbors move in, her solitude begins to unravel in tender, sometimes humorous ways.

Why it helps: This novel is perfect for those living with grief-born depression or quiet emotional withdrawal. It shows how even the smallest cracks in our armour can be openings for light. Gently redemptive and deeply kind.

The Reading List by Sara Nisha Adams

When lonely widower Mukesh finds a crumpled reading list at his local library, he begins working through the titles—and forms a surprising friendship with Aleisha, a troubled teenage library clerk. Through fiction, both characters begin to make sense of grief, anxiety, and the parts of themselves they'd long shut away.

Why it helps: Because it is a story about how books—and the people who love them—can save us. Gentle, intergenerational, and quietly luminous, it's a tribute to the healing power of words and the unexpected ways in which life can offer companionship, even when we feel most alone.

The Mind That Wouldn't Settle

Some days, the sky inside your chest
feels too heavy to lift.
Even the light stings.
Even the silence hums.
You make the coffee, wash the dishes,
answer the questions—
but some part of you has curled inward,
too tired to come out.

This is not failure.
This is the body's cry for gentleness.

The world may call it weakness,
but I call it sacred—
the soft alert that says:
You've carried too much for too long,
without enough hands to hold you.

You do not owe anyone your sparkle.
You do not need to earn rest.
Even the sun disappears behind clouds sometimes,
and no one questions its worth.

So if all you did today
was breathe through the weight—
you did enough.

Emotional Silencing

Unspoken– Breaking the Spell of Emotional Silencing

There are wounds that don't bruise, don't scream, don't even show. They leave a woman standing in a room, quiet, composed, and unable to say what she knows. Not because she lacks the words, but because she's been trained, over years or lifetimes, to hold them in.

This chapter is for the woman who was told to "calm down" when what she really needed was to be heard. For the professional who learned that only logic is credible–and that intuition must be repackaged in data to be taken seriously. For the daughter who absorbed every subtle cue–every tone, glance, and sigh– that taught her some feelings are too much. Too loud. Too inconvenient. Too dramatic.

This is for the woman whose rage became migraines. Whose grief became insomnia. Whose truth became a clenched jaw, a kind email, a spiritual bypass.

We live in a world that often celebrates emotional literacy in theory but penalizes it in practice. Women are praised for their compassion but discouraged from naming their anger. Encouraged to nurture but shamed when they set a boundary. And so we internalize a deep, patterned silencing–a subtle erosion of emotional truth in service of "fitting in," "keeping the peace," or simply surviving.

But fiction, blessed fiction, doesn't ask us to be quiet. It lets us feel without apology.

It gives us characters who cry in parking lots, who scream at the wrong moment, who ache with longing, who carry generational silence in their skin. It shows us what happens when we suppress—and what becomes possible when we don't. The stories we read can be mirrors. They remind us that just because a woman is composed doesn't mean she is at peace. That emotional honesty is not weakness; it is courage. And that feeling deeply is not something to hide. It's something to honor.

Let this chapter be a warm hand on your back. Let it be a space to remember what you've muted. Let it be a safe haven where your feelings—your truest, most authentic emotions—are not only accepted but honored. In stories, we find the healing that silence could never provide. We are invited into spaces where we can simply be, feel everything without apology, and reclaim the voice that we've buried in the hopes of fitting in.

And if a story brings tears, or goosebumps, or a surprising surge of emotion, you're not overreacting. You're remembering. You're reconnecting with the parts of yourself that were never meant to be muted. And this time, they will not be.

When Spiritual Language Silences Truth

There's a kind of silence that doesn't come from suppression—it comes dressed in light. The kind that tells us to forgive before we've grieved. To be grateful before we've acknowledged the loss. To rise above, let go, move on—when what we need is to sit down and feel. This is the quiet harm of spiritual bypassing.

It happens when spiritual language is used to avoid, deflect, or diminish pain. When phrases like "everything happens for a reason" or "just stay positive" are offered not as comfort but as escape routes—from discomfort, from vulnerability, from emotional truth. It often comes with good intentions. But the impact is still silencing.

Bypassing doesn't just happen in spiritual circles. It happens in workplaces, families, friendships. It happens every time someone's anger is called unspiritual. Every time a boundary is labeled unkind. Every time the language of "light and love" is used to avoid the necessary darkness. Emotional honesty is not a failure of faith; it is the foundation of it. We cannot heal what we will not face. We cannot integrate what we're told to skip.

Let this chapter—and the stories it contains—be a reminder that there is nothing wrong with feeling deeply, naming what hurts, or walking through the fire instead of around it. Real healing is not a detour. It's a descent. And we are not meant to go alone—or in silence.

Book Friends

These are stories of emotional truth that could not be spoken—until they were. Each book in this section explores what happens when voices are muted, feelings are buried, and women are taught to make themselves smaller than their full emotional lives. Some of these characters quietly unravel. Others quietly rebel. All illuminate the cost of emotional silencing—and the power of reclaiming one's voice.

Never Let Me Go by Kazuo Ishiguro

A quietly devastating novel that shows how emotional suppression can be institutionalized—and how tenderness finds its way through.

> *Why it helps:* Because it reveals how systemic silence shapes identity—and how even in the bleakest settings, humanity resists erasure.

A Thousand Acres by Jane Smiley

A modern retelling of King Lear set on an Iowa farm, this novel uncovers the generational layers of silence, trauma, and unspoken history within a family.

> *Why it helps:* Because it names the cost of silence passed down, and the quiet bravery it takes to break that chain.

The House of Mirth by Edith Wharton

A searing portrait of a woman navigating rigid social codes in turn-of-the-century New York.

> *Why it helps:* Because it lays bare the emotional and social cost of denying complexity and truth in a woman's life.

Women Talking by Miriam Toews
A fictional retelling of real-life events where Mennonite women gather in secret to decide their response to years of sexual abuse.

> *Why it helps:* Because it honors the radical courage of women finding voice after silence. It speaks to collective truth-telling, spiritual autonomy, and what it means to reclaim your agency in a system built to suppress it.

The Wisdom of Your Body by Hillary L. McBride *(nonfiction)*
A powerful exploration of how trauma, shame, and societal expectations disconnect women from their bodies and feelings—and how reconnecting with our full emotional selves is a path to healing. Drawing on psychology, lived experience, and somatic practices, McBride offers a compassionate guide to becoming emotionally whole.

> *Why it helps:* Because it speaks directly to the internalized silencing so many women endure. This book affirms that emotions live in the body, and that honoring them is not indulgent—it's necessary for healing and self-trust.

The Gentle Mask of Light

She was taught to lower her voice—
to be polite, not piercing.
To nod, not question.
To smile, not feel.

But the ache built slowly.
A weight behind the ribs.
A knowing in the throat
that silence could no longer hold.

So one day,
she spoke anyway.

Not loudly—
but clearly.
Not perfectly—
but truthfully.

And in that moment,
the world didn't shatter.
It shifted.

**Because one woman's voice
can be a beginning.**

Section 3: Belonging & Disconnection

We are born with the ache to belong.

To be seen. To be known.
To find a place where we don't have to explain
or shrink or hide what hurts.

But life doesn't always grant us that ease.

Sometimes, we are strangers in our own families.
Sometimes, the world tells us we don't fit the mold—
and then asks us to thank it for letting us stay.

This section is for anyone
who has ever stood at the edge
of belonging.

For those who have felt the silence
of a room that should have welcomed them,
or the absence of a love that should have stayed.

These stories offer more than connection.
They offer *recognition*.
Not just of who are you—
but of all the places you've searched for home.

Family Dysfunction

Unraveling the Knots

Not all wounds come from strangers. Some of the deepest ones are made at the dinner table.

Family is often idealized as a place of belonging—but for many, it is where the confusion begins. Where love and loyalty become tangled with silence, shame, and control. Where emotional needs go unmet, or worse, are dismissed entirely.

Dysfunction doesn't always wear dramatic clothing. Sometimes, it's quiet. A lack of listening. A pattern of blame. An invisible script passed down through generations: *Don't speak. Don't feel. Don't disrupt.*

And yet, within the chaos of broken dynamics, there are still slivers of love—often too complex to name, too conditional to trust. That's what makes family dysfunction so disorienting. It's not the absence of connection but the inconsistency of it. The ache of wanting closeness with people who cannot—or will not—meet you in the truth.

This section is for anyone who grew up walking on eggshells. For the ones who became the peacekeepers, the fixers, the ones who took on too much, too soon. For those who were scapegoated, gaslit, or quietly erased.

Fiction can name what was never said aloud. It can help us locate ourselves outside the roles we were assigned. And sometimes, it can even show us what it means to love without losing ourselves.

These stories don't just depict dysfunction; they dismantle it, offering new blueprints for relationships, healing, and chosen family.

Book Friends

These stories don't tidy up the past—they illuminate it, one messy thread at a time. Let them help you name what hurt, hold what still lingers, and imagine what healing might look like from here.

The Most Fun We Ever Had by Claire Lombardo
Spanning fifty years, this sweeping novel follows four adult sisters whose seemingly perfect parents cast long shadows over their choices, relationships, and sense of identity. Rich with family tension, layered secrets, and emotional entanglement.

> *Why it helps:* Because it shows that even tightly knit families can carry tightly held pain. This novel validates the complexity of love in flawed systems—and invites us to untangle identity from expectation.

This Is Where I Leave You by Jonathan Tropper
When their father dies, four adult siblings return to their childhood home to sit shiva under one roof. What unfolds is a darkly comic, brutally honest reckoning with past wounds, unresolved rivalries, and long-suppressed truths.

> *Why it helps:* Because sometimes, the truth comes out sideways. This story uses humour to soften hard edges and reminds us that dysfunction doesn't mean we're unlovable—it means we're human, and we're still healing.

Ask Again, Yes by Mary Beth Keane
Two neighboring families are ripped apart by a shocking act of violence, yet their lives remain intertwined for decades. With sensitivity and nuance, this novel explores mental illness, forgiveness, and how children inherit—and sometimes transcend—the emotional legacies of their parents.

> *Why it helps:* Because it speaks to the long arc of healing. This novel gently explores how trauma lingers—and how love can still grow in its shadow.

The Turner House by Angela Flournoy

Thirteen siblings return to their Detroit family home as their mother's health declines and their childhood house faces foreclosure. With heart and humour, this novel offers a deeply human look at memory, inheritance, and the ghosts—literal and figurative—that inhabit families.

> ***Why it helps:*** Because it affirms that family stories are both burden and balm. This novel holds space for laughter, grief, and the complicated grace of coming home to what shaped us.

Everything I Never Told You by Celeste Ng

When the beloved daughter of a Chinese American family is found dead, long-held secrets unravel as each family member confronts the silent pressures, buried grief, and unspoken expectations that have shaped their lives.

> ***Why it helps:*** Because it reveals how silence can fracture a family—and how the things we don't say often shape us more than the ones we do. This novel holds space for those raised in households of quiet hurt and invisible rules.

Alone in a Crowd

You laugh at the right time.
Show up with wine.
Text back with hearts and emojis.
Your feed is full—
but your soul feels empty.

You're not dramatic. Not needy.
Just tired of being unseen
in places where everyone is looking,
but no one really sees.

You go to the party. You smile in photos.
You tell yourself this is connection—
but something aches
for a deeper yes.
A hand on your shoulder.
A voice that says,
"I'm here—no mask, no scroll, no hurry."

So tonight, turn off the noise.
Let a story be your witness.
Let a character say
what you haven't dared admit.

You are not alone.
You're just hungry
for real.

Loneliness & Isolation

The Ache of Absence

Loneliness is not just the absence of people; it's the absence of *presence*. Of being truly seen, heard, and valued. You can be surrounded by family, partnered in love, or part of a bustling group—and still feel utterly alone.

Today, loneliness is a quiet epidemic. Not just among the elderly, as we've long assumed, but across every age group. Teenagers with hundreds of followers feel unseen. Young mothers feel invisible. Midlife professionals scroll late at night, wondering why the curated beauty on their screens only deepens their ache. And yes—our elders. Those who gave, taught, built, and raised now spend entire days in silence, unseen by the world they helped create.

We were not made to live like this.

Our culture has confused connection with contact. We think a "like" is a conversation. We confuse proximity for intimacy. And in the race for efficiency, we've lost the art of lingering, of asking real questions, and of showing up when it's inconvenient.

Loneliness isn't always dramatic. It's quiet. Subtle. It settles into the creases of the day—

When no one asks how you really are.

When your phone lights up, but no one says your name out loud.

When you realize you can't remember the last time someone touched your hand with tenderness.

And it is especially brutal for the elderly. Many of our elders—those who once lived in rich webs of family and neighborhood—now sit in rooms filled only with flickering screens and the noise of daytime television. Their memories are intact, but their calendars are blank. Their wisdom remains, but no one asks. They carry stories, histories, love—and yet their greatest fear is not death but being forgotten *while still alive.*

Loneliness doesn't discriminate, but it *deepens* in the spaces where we've stopped paying attention.

This section of the book is for anyone who has ever felt like their presence doesn't matter. It does. It always has.

And it's also a gentle call to all of us—

Check on the quiet ones.
Write a letter.
Ask better questions.
Don't let convenience replace care.

Because one day, we may find ourselves on the other side of that silence, waiting for a knock that never comes.

Book Friends

Loneliness wears many faces. It can look like a quiet older man eating alone at a café, or a young woman posting smiling selfies from a room that feels hollow. It can visit after loss, after change, or even in the middle of a full, busy life. Sometimes, it comes not from being alone but from being unseen.

These stories offer companionship in all its forms: Unexpected friendships. Solitary lives with flickers of grace. Tender reminders that even in our loneliest chapters, we are never truly alone. Sometimes, all it takes is a story to sit with us—and gently lead us back to ourselves.

Convenience Store Woman by Sayaka Murata

A quietly powerful novel about a woman who feels most at home in the predictable rhythms of her job. A meditation on loneliness, social norms, and the courage it takes to live differently.

> *Why it helps:* Because it affirms the quiet strength of being yourself. This story invites us to honour the beauty of lives lived outside the script—and the dignity of solitude by choice.

The Housekeeper and the Professor by Yōko Ogawa

A mathematical genius with a memory that resets every 80 minutes forms a touching, unlikely friendship with his housekeeper and her son. A gentle, poetic novel about loneliness, kindness, and small moments of grace.

> *Why it helps:* Because it offers companionship in small doses of wonder. This story reminds us that connection doesn't have to be permanent to be meaningful.

Frankenstein by Mary Shelley

Beyond the horror, this is a story of isolation—of a creature, rejected by its maker and the world, longing to belong. A gothic meditation on alienation, identity, and the human need for connection

> *Why it helps:* Because it gives voice to the outsider. Frankenstein's creature speaks to anyone who has ever felt rejected, misjudged, or unloved for simply existing.

An Unnecessary Woman by Rabih Alameddine

A solitary woman in her seventies lives quietly in Beirut, surrounded by books, memory, and the steady ritual of translating literature that no one will ever read. She speaks little, engages less—but her interior world is vast, luminous, and full of insight.

Why it helps: Because it affirms that solitude is not always a wound—it can be a sanctuary. A meditation on aging, creativity, and self-containment, this novel honours the beauty of a life lived deeply and inwardly. For those who have ever felt invisible, it says: Your inner world is enough. And it matters.

Luster by Raven Leilani

A sharp, poetic novel about a young woman navigating isolation, identity, and intimacy in a world that promises connection but delivers confusion. Bold, aching, and deeply honest about what it means to feel alone in plain sight.

Why it helps: Because it names the loneliness that hides beneath performance. This novel dares to say what many feel and few admit—that being seen doesn't always mean being known.

The Flatshare by Beth O'Leary

A charming, unexpected love story between two strangers who share a flat (and a bed) but never meet. Through the notes they leave, they begin to truly see one another. A modern antidote to loneliness, reminding us that intimacy can bloom even in strange arrangements.

Why it helps: Because it affirms that connection can begin with the smallest gesture. This story reminds us that being seen starts with being real—even on paper.

The Ones We Leave in Quiet Rooms

They do not ask for much.
Just time.
A voice.
A moment of *you*.

They once held your hand,
picked you up,
taught you how to stand.
Now they sit—
silent,
in rooms that buzz with television
but ache with absence.

Their friends are gone.
Their limbs are slow.
The world has become a blur
of days that all look the same.

And still—
they remember.
The birthdays they never missed.
The meals they cooked from memory.
The ways they gave,
again and again,
without asking for thanks.
But now,
their names are on calendars
instead of in conversations.
Their voices echo in empty kitchens.

And their greatest fear
is not death–
but being forgotten
while still alive.

So bring them a book.
Read them a story.
Sit with them in the pauses.
Let fiction do what we've forgotten how to do–
make time.
Make meaning.
Make company.

Because one day,
it will be *us*
waiting for the knock
that never comes.

LGBTQ+

Rejection & the Right to Belong

Why This Chapter Exists

This chapter was born one afternoon while I was listening to Calum Scott sing *Boys in the Street*. A song so tender, so devastating, it brought me to stillness. In it, a boy is rejected by his father for being gay. He spends his life just wanting to be seen—not changed, not saved, just seen. And though his father accepts him on his deathbed, the moment comes too late to undo the ache.

That song stayed with me. Not just for the story it told—but for how many people I know, how many readers I imagine, who have lived their own version of it. A version where love came with conditions. Where truth came at a cost. Where family—the place meant to hold you—became the place that broke you.

This section is for them. For the unchosen. For those told they didn't belong, yet somehow chose to stay—on this earth, in their truth, and in the quiet revolution of becoming.

This chapter isn't about labels. It's about **loss**—the ache of being pushed away—for telling the truth, for stepping into your voice, for simply being yourself.

Some rejections are loud—doors slammed, names erased. Others are quieter: the distance that grows, the silence that hardens, the celebration that never comes. This kind of grief doesn't come with rituals. It comes with birthdays missed, invitations never sent, and a name no longer spoken aloud.

Whether your story is shaped by family, faith, culture, or fear—this section is for you.

For those who've been told they don't belong, these pages offer something gentler: not just reflection, but recognition.

The Unchosen Child

There is a particular kind of grief that doesn't come with flowers or sympathy cards. It comes with silence. With being left out of family photos. With birthdays unacknowledged. With the phrase, "We just can't accept this."

This is the grief of the unchosen child.

The one who came out—and was cast out. The one who told the truth—and was told to leave. The one who changed their name, their body, their future—and in doing so, lost the people who were supposed to love them unconditionally.

Sometimes, the rejection is overt: a slammed door, a shouted shame, or a mother who says, "You're no longer my daughter." Other times, it's quieter. A creeping distance. A refusal to ask questions. A name never spoken again.

This grief is not just about loss—it's about betrayal. Because love, real love, is supposed to say, "No matter what." But for too many, there was a *what* they could not survive.

And yet, many unchosen children still choose to live. To love. To build new families made not of blood but of tenderness. To write themselves back into the world after being erased.

This section is for them. For those who have sat through holiday dinners where their name was never mentioned. For those who weren't hugged at graduations. For those whose weddings went unattended.

You are not unlovable. You are not wrong. You are not alone. You were never meant to stay in a story where your light had to dim so others could stay comfortable. The love that could not hold you was never the measure of your worth.

You are not the broken one. You are the brave one.

Book Friends
Orlando by Virginia Woolf
A gender-defying classic about identity, transformation, and love across centuries. Boldly ahead of its time, it celebrates becoming oneself beyond social norms or expectations.

Why it helps: Because it affirms that identity can be fluid, joyful, and unconstrained by time or tradition. A beautiful mirror for those still shaping their own truth.

This Is How It Always Is by **Laurie Frankel**

A warm, moving novel about a family navigating life with a transgender daughter. Explores the complexities of unconditional love, secrecy, and the freedom of living openly.

Why it helps: Because it offers hope through messiness. This novel affirms that acceptance is not perfection—it's love in motion.

The Miseducation of Cameron Post by **Emily M. Danforth**

After losing her parents, a young girl is sent to a religious conversion camp. A powerful coming-of-age story about shame, survival, and the resilience of queer youth.

Why it helps: Because it shines a light on systems of harm—and the sacred act of surviving them. A reminder that you are never wrong for being real.

Detransition, Baby by **Torrey Peters**

Three women—trans, cis, and formerly trans—navigate the complexities of identity, parenthood, and belonging. Sharp, funny, and deeply layered in its treatment of chosen and unchosen family.

Why it helps: Because it invites every facet of identity into the room. Complex, messy, and human, this is a novel for anyone building family on their own terms.

We Are Okay by Nina LaCour

A lyrical young adult novel about a college student estranged from family and grieving a secret loss. Quiet, emotionally rich, and full of longing for connection.

Why it helps: Because it speaks softly to grief that has no name. A companion for those navigating distance, silence, and the ache of absence.

Nevada by Imogen Binnie

A raw, punk-infused novel about a trans woman searching for meaning, identity, and connection after a breakup. Gritty and honest, it captures transition as both interior and societal upheaval.

Why it helps: Because it doesn't sanitize the struggle. It gives voice to confusion, resilience, and messy becoming.

Love in the Big City by Sang Young Park

A young queer man navigates love, illness, and nightlife in modern Seoul. Irreverent, tender, and sharply funny, it captures the strange intimacy of urban life.

Why it helps: Because it shows queerness as vibrantly lived—not always heroic, but always deeply human.

This Is How You Lose the Time War by **Amal El-Mohtar & Max Gladstone**

Two rival agents in a war across time leave secret letters—and fall in love. Lyrical, poetic, and wildly original, it's a meditation on connection across every boundary.

> *Why it helps:* Because it proves that love transcends structure. This story is a literary spell, reminding us that connection can thrive even in impossible places.

Last Night at the Telegraph Club by **Malinda Lo**

Set in 1950s Chinatown, a young Chinese American girl discovers both her queerness and her courage. Historical fiction with a beating heart—quiet, defiant, and beautifully researched.

> *Why it helps:* Because it honours quiet bravery. This novel offers the courage of a whisper—a soft coming-out story that still shakes the walls of conformity.

Fun Home by **Alison Bechdel** *(nonfiction)*

A graphic memoir exploring Bechdel's coming out, her closeted father's double life, and the silence that shaped their family. Brilliant, literary, and heartbreaking in its honesty.

> *Why it helps:* Because it captures the pain of silence and the liberation of speaking anyway. A balm for anyone whose truth was met with absence.

Section 4: Life Transitions & Identity Shifts

There are seasons that arrive without warning—when the ground beneath you moves and nothing feels certain anymore.

Roles change. Chapters close. Children grow. Parents fade. Jobs end. The body shifts.

And suddenly, you're standing in a space you didn't plan for— no longer who you were, not yet who you're becoming.

This section holds stories of that in-between. Of motherhood— messy, miraculous, or missing. Of aging not as decline, but as deepening. Of caregiving born from love, not always freely given. Of letting go of one identity to discover another.

These are not stories of endings. They are stories of becoming— of women who reshaped their lives because something within them whispered: *You're allowed to change.*

Let these pages offer company as you step across your own quiet thresholds.

Motherhood

The Many Rooms of Motherhood

Motherhood is not a single role. It is a shifting constellation of identities—nurturer, protector, teacher, mirror, guide, soul companion. It is a job with no manual, no finish line, and, often, no room to rest.

It asks us to stretch our hearts until they ache. To stay soft even when we are bone-tired. To let go even as we hold on.

Motherhood is love with no off switch. It is waking in the night to rock a sick child, missing pieces of yourself while building someone else, and wondering, often in silence, who you were before all this began.

There are seasons when a mother becomes invisible—when her needs shrink behind school lunches, medical appointments, tears at bedtime, and the hum of survival. And yet within that invisibility, something eternal pulses: devotion. A kind of fierce, ordinary, world-shaping devotion.

This section honours both the tenderness and the tenacity of motherhood. The quiet resilience. The unfinished cups of coffee. The stretching and breaking and becoming.

Fiction helps us name what is often unspoken. Stories of mothers—biological, chosen, lost, or rediscovered—remind us that mothering isn't about perfection. It's about presence. It's about returning, again and again, even when you're running on empty.

Motherhood may be universal, but each journey through it is uniquely sacred.

Let this section be a breath. A recognition. A small altar for all that has been given, held, carried, and forgiven.

As Anne Lamott once wrote:

"There really are places in the heart you don't even know exist until you love a child."

Book Friends

Motherhood is not one story. It is a thousand silent threads—tender, tangled, taut. It is devotion and disorientation, the giving away of sleep, time, and sometimes even self. It is also power. The quiet, shape-shifting kind—capable of building worlds and breaking generational spells with a whisper or a scream.

These stories do not offer a single truth. They offer windows into the ache. The beauty. The rage. The choice. The forgetting and the remembering. The woman before the child, and the one who rises after.

Room by Emma Donoghue

A powerful story of a mother's love and resourcefulness, told from the perspective of her five-year-old son.

> *Why it helps:* This novel reveals the fierce, intuitive power of maternal protection—even under unimaginable conditions. Told through a child's eyes, it reminds readers of the emotional sanctuary a mother creates, and how love can outgrow even captivity.

The Light Between Oceans by M.L. Stedman

A haunting novel about longing, moral conflict, and the choices that shape a mother's soul.

> *Why it helps:* This book explores the aching complexity of motherhood when life refuses easy answers. It invites reflection on what makes someone a mother—and how grief, love, and conscience can become entwined in the choices women carry.

Little Fires Everywhere by Celeste Ng
Explores complex questions of motherhood, race, privilege, and the meaning of "real" parenting.

> *Why it helps:* Ng's novel holds up a mirror to the layered expectations placed on mothers—especially across lines of class, culture, and identity. It encourages compassionate reflection on the many forms love can take, and who gets to define "good" mothering.

The Lost Daughter by Elena Ferrante
A psychological portrait of a woman reckoning with her own past as both daughter and mother.

> *Why it helps:* Ferrante's fearless honesty opens space for women to name the ambivalence, guilt, and longing that often go unspoken in the maternal journey. It speaks to those reclaiming their own identity, especially after years of emotional caretaking.

Nightbitch by Rachel Yoder
A surreal and feral meditation on the transformation of identity in early motherhood—raw, wild, and unapologetic.

> *Why it helps:* This daring novel cracks open the polished image of motherhood to reveal its primal, creative chaos. It gives permission to feel rage, desire, and magic—all the emotions often buried under societal expectations.

Let the Rest Find You

You don't have to lie down.
You don't have to light a candle,
or journal,
or slow your breath like they say.

Just let the stillness
find a way in.
Let it slip between the emails.
Let it lean against the fridge
while you pack lunches again.
Let it rest its head on your shoulder
when the baby won't sleep.

You don't have to name it peace.
You don't have to earn it.
But when it comes—
and it will—
in the hot shower
or the held gaze,
in the moment no one is asking
and you don't need to answer—
Let it stay.

Let it remind you
that you were never meant
to carry everything
alone.

And that even if you won't rest
for yourself,
rest will still try to find you.

Aging

Still Vital: Celebrating Aging

This is not elderhood through the lens of legacy or spiritual wisdom—that comes later. This is the aging of right now. The one where your mind is sharper than ever, your voice is clearer, and your joy no longer seeks permission.

They say aging is a quiet thing. But that's only what it looks like from the outside. Inside, it's anything but quiet. It's vivid. Confrontational. Sacred. It's a slow becoming and a tender unbecoming. A shedding of masks. A rewriting of worth. A second birth, but this time—we're awake.

And yet, for many women, aging brings with it a strange kind of invisibility. Not because we've dimmed, but because the world has stopped looking. I hear it often: "So... you've retired?" As if vitality comes with an expiry date. As if creativity, sensuality, and purpose are only for the young. As if presence can be measured by pace or productivity.

But here's what they don't see: Inside, I don't feel diminished. I feel *essential*.

Yes, my body has softened. My mirror has shifted. But my voice? It's clearer. My wisdom? Deeper. The self-doubt that haunted me in my twenties has left the room. And the girl I once pitied for her flaws, I now grieve for, because she didn't yet know she was already enough.

This culture may be obsessed with youth, but the truth is quieter and more enduring: Older people, research shows, are often happier. Why? Because we've stopped performing. Because we know what peace feels like—and we won't trade it for polish. Because we've come home to the essence of who we are.

These later years are not a decline. They are a distillation. A return—not to who we were, but to who we've always been.

So, this section is for the women who no longer chase relevance but embody resonance. Who are no longer interested in being looked at but long to be *understood*. Who feel most alive just as the world begins to look away.

We are not past our prime. *We are finally in it.*

These stories reflect that back to us. And so does she—the archetype we've been taught to fear but are finally learning to revere.

Book Friends

These stories reflect aging not as diminishment but as distillation. They center women who are no longer chasing relevance but embodying resonance. With clarity, humor, sensuality, and truth, each novel offers a reminder: we are not past our prime—we are finally in it.

Tirra Lirra by the River by Jessica Anderson

At 70, Nora returns to her childhood home after a life abroad, reflecting on her past with equal parts detachment and tenderness.

> ***Why it helps:*** Because it gently honors the private narratives of aging—and reminds us that clarity often comes later, and peace arrives in quiet waves.

A Spool of Blue Thread by Anne Tyler

Spanning generations, this family saga threads through memory, miscommunication, and the small domestic rhythms that shape a life.

> ***Why it helps:*** Because it treats aging with grace and truth—neither feared nor romanticized, just fully lived within the folds of everyday existence.

The Stone Angel by **Margaret Laurence**
A Canadian classic exploring the interior world of Hagar Shipley, a proud and often difficult elderly woman confronting her past. As her body weakens, her memories sharpen—revealing a lifetime of love, loss, and stubbornness in equal measure.

> *Why it helps:* Because it captures the ache and pride of aging. Hagar's story reminds us that even in our final chapters, we are still trying to be understood—and still capable of reckoning with the selves we used to be.

Margaret's New Look by **Katherine Ashenburg**
At 82, Margaret shocks her friends and family by reinventing her life—from her wardrobe to her desires—and proving it's never too late to disrupt expectations.

> *Why it helps:* Because it celebrates liberation in old age, challenging ageism with wit, agency, and unapologetic self-expression.

The Wonder and Happiness of Being Old by **Sophy Burnham** *(nonfiction)*
A warm, reflective collection of unsent letters exploring the unexpected beauty of growing older. Burnham writes with humour, grace, and deep insight about freedom, perspective, and the quiet joys that often arrive with age.

> *Why it helps:* For anyone feeling unsure about aging, this book offers comfort and clarity. It reframes later life as a time of truth, peace, and becoming—rather than decline.

The Disappearing Woman Myth

She was visible—until she wasn't.

One day, she noticed that people stopped making eye contact. That her ideas were echoed back to her as someone else's. That servers offered the wine list to the younger woman beside her.

She hadn't changed. She had ripened. But the world had decided: *You've had your moment.*

This is the myth: that a woman's worth peaks with youth. That visibility belongs to the smooth, the fast, the pleasing.

But you are not here to disappear. You are here to deepen. To become seen not for how you look but for who you've become.

She Wasn't Done

They said she'd softened—
but really, she'd sharpened.
Her edges were no longer hidden
beneath the need to please.
She stopped apologizing
for the echo in her voice
or the quiet certainty in her gaze.

She wore silver like armour.
Laughed without asking.
Took her coffee slow
and her solitude sacred.

She no longer mistook silence for shame,
nor slowness for decline.
She knew the value of pause.
Of listening.
Of speaking only when the truth was ready.

They thought she'd fade.
But she bloomed sideways—
through cracks,
through stillness,
through the wild garden
of her own becoming.

She wasn't done.
She was just
finally uninterrupted.

Finding Purpose (Post-Retirement)

Not Done, But Free

Some women enter retirement with a plan—travel, hobbies, rest. Others arrive quietly stunned. No more emails. No more titles. No more structured hours or identity built into a role. And for many, especially those who didn't choose it, retirement doesn't feel like freedom. It feels like erasure.

You were needed. Then you weren't. And no one told you what to do with the ache of that.

This section is for the woman who spent her life giving—at work, at home, in her community—and now finds herself with open time and no map. It's for the woman who loved her work and didn't want to stop, but who was pushed out because of a number on a birth certificate. It's for anyone wondering: *Is it too late to begin again? Is there something still meant for me?*

And let's be clear: there is no "retirement" from voice, from joy, from calling. You are not finished. You are simply *unconstrained* for the first time in years. That doesn't mean you know what to do next. But it does mean you get to choose.

Purpose after retirement doesn't have to look like a grand project or reinvention. Sometimes, it's rediscovering your own rhythm. Sometimes, it's saying "yes" to something small and sacred. Sometimes, it's writing the book, planting the garden, mentoring one person, starting the walk that becomes a pilgrimage.

There is no formula, only this truth: *You are still becoming.* And this next chapter? It may just be the one that is most fully yours.

Book Friends
For the woman who is only just beginning

Retirement is a word the world uses to close doors. But for many women, it is not an ending—it is a reclamation. Of time. Of truth. Of joy not filtered through someone else's expectations.

This stage of life is not defined by age. It is defined by space. By the courage to ask: *What do I want now?* By the freedom to say: *This chapter is mine.*

These stories are companions for the path ahead. They don't all begin with clarity. Some begin with loss, with boredom, or with disbelief. But they arrive, eventually, at purpose. Sometimes in the form of friendship. Sometimes rebellion. Sometimes quiet contentment. Each one is a reminder: *You are not done. You are just free.*

The Lido by Libby Page
A shy young journalist teams up with an elderly woman to save their beloved local pool, uncovering stories of resilience, loss, and unexpected connection.

> *Why it helps:* Because it honours legacy and intergenerational friendship—and reminds us that meaning often returns through community, not isolation.

Mrs. Palfrey at the Claremont by Elizabeth Taylor
A widowed woman settles into a residential hotel for the elderly and finds companionship in a young writer, rewriting what it means to be visible in later life.

> *Why it helps:* Because it validates the emotional richness of aging and the quiet ache for recognition and dignity that lives beneath every generation.

An Elderly Lady Is Up to No Good by **Helene Tursten**

Maud is 88, lives alone in a lovely Gothenburg apartment, and has no interest in giving up her independence—or putting up with anyone's nonsense. With dry wit and a darkly comic twist, this collection of linked stories shows how Maud handles intrusions with... creative solutions.

> ***Why it helps:*** Because it turns the idea of the "invisible old woman" on its head. This sharp, subversive book reminds us that autonomy, wit, and purpose don't fade with age—they sharpen.

The Thursday Murder Club by **Richard Osman**

In a quiet retirement village, four sharp-witted seniors meet weekly to solve cold cases—until a real murder lands on their doorstep. Clever, charming, and full of heart, this bestseller blends mystery with mischief and unexpected camaraderie.

> ***Why it helps:*** Because it shows that retirement doesn't mean irrelevance. It's a warm reminder that intellect, intuition, and impact don't retire when the job does. Purpose may just come with tea, banter, and a mystery to solve.

The Chapter She Writes Now

She stepped out of the title
and into the stillness.
No meetings. No inbox.
No nameplate on the door.

At first, it felt like falling—
into absence, into air.
But slowly,
the space became something else:
a blank page
with no deadline.

She planted a garden.
She said "no" without guilt.
She wandered,
not to get somewhere—
but to remember who she was
before becoming what others needed.

And in that wandering,
she did not get lost.
She got free.

This is not the end of her story.
This is the chapter
she gets to write
with her own hand.

Caregiving

In the Wake of Love: The Caregiver's Truth

There are kinds of courage we rarely speak of. The kind that wakes at 2 a.m. The kind that tracks appointments, prescriptions, and vital signs without ever tracking your own needs. The kind that redefines what love looks like when the person you care for no longer recognizes you—or themselves.

Caregiving is often called a gift. But that word, spoken too soon, can sting. Because when you're in it—when the walls close in, when your life shrinks around someone else's decline—what you feel is not gifted. What you feel is tethered. Grieving. Lonely. Exhausted. And so rarely seen.

This chapter is written by someone who gets it.

For nearly ten years, I cared for my mother through the long arc of her declining health. During that time, I also took on the care of my father, from whom I had been estranged for over a decade. After separating from his second wife, he had no one else. And so, despite everything he had been, I showed up. I became his caregiver for four years—while still caring for my mother.

In those years, I lost count of the sacrifices. The rescheduled plans. The sleepless nights. The doctors who dismissed. The friends who disappeared. And I lost count, too, of how many people tried to spiritualize the experience. "Find the gift," they'd say. "It's all for a reason."

But caregiving is not something you rise above. It is something you live through. And some days, surviving it *is* the gift.

This section is for the women who stayed. Who cancelled or shortened trips, gave up jobs, ate meals standing, cried in the car. It's for those who were everything for someone else—and nothing for themselves. It's for the women who were expected to be saints and settled for being strong. And for those who feel that no one truly saw what it cost.

You are not alone. And you deserve stories that reflect what you carried.

Book Friends
The Dutch House by Ann Patchett
A powerful sibling story wrapped in the long arc of caregiving and role reversal.

> *Why it helps:* For those navigating family dynamics while caring for aging parents, this novel explores what is inherited—emotionally and practically—when we step into the roles others once held. It's a reminder that the house you return to—literally or metaphorically—is often where the hardest reckonings and most unexpected loyalties live.

The One Hundred Years of Lenni and Margot by Marianne Cronin
A young girl and an elderly woman form a bond in a hospital that becomes a space for joy, honesty, and reflection.

> *Why it helps:* This novel reminds caregivers of the small beauties that exist alongside the pain—and the dignity in shared presence.

The Japanese Lover by Isabel Allende
Spanning decades and told through the friendship between a young caregiver and an elderly woman in a San Francisco care home, this novel unveils a secret love story, generational trauma, and the slow surrender of independence.

Why it helps: Because it explores aging not as decline but as revelation. Through its tender intergenerational lens, the novel affirms the dignity of memory, the ache of letting go, and the quiet power of being witnessed at life's end.

Can't We Talk About Something More Pleasant? by Roz Chast *(nonfiction)*
A memoir in cartoons about aging parents, denial, and the uncomfortable truths no one wants to say out loud.

Why it helps: This book makes you laugh *and* cry. It's brutally real—and sometimes, that's exactly what you need.

Feeding My Mother by Jann Arden *(nonfiction)*
Canadian singer Jann Arden writes with rawness and humour about caring for her mother with Alzheimer's.

Why it helps: Honest and unfiltered, this book gives voice to the emotional rollercoaster of loving someone through their decline, without romanticizing the process.

The Caregiver's Quiet

No one sees the nights.
The calls at 2 a.m.–
your heart racing
before your feet hit the floor,
keys grabbed with trembling hands
because they fell.
Again.

And the guilt arrives
before you even do.
Your life–
a calendar of obligation.
Appointments. Pills. Groceries.
A tether, not a rhythm.

You once moved freely.
Now the world moves through you
without asking.

You love them. You do.
But some days–
you want to vanish into silence.
Not forever.
Just long enough
to hear your own breath
in a room with no questions,
no collapsing into strength.

They say caregiving is noble.
But nobility doesn't explain
why you lose your temper
over a sock,
then cry behind the bathroom door.

You know they don't want to need you.
You know they feel the burden.
And you wish you didn't feel
so heavy with it all.

You are exhausted,
not because you don't care—
but because you do.
So deeply. So constantly. So invisibly.
Still—
you make breakfast. You help them dress.
You smile through clenched compassion.
You love with blistered hands
and a splintered heart.

But here's what no one told you:
You matter, too.
Not just as a helper.
Not just as a role.
As a person. A soul.

You're allowed to rest.
To step away.
To say "Not today"
and still mean love.

Section 5: Resilience & Renewal

You made it through
what they thought would break you.

Maybe you didn't rise in a blaze of glory—
but you rose.

You kept going when no one was watching.
You stitched your life
back together with breath, and time,
and the smallest scraps of hope.

This section is a testament
to that kind of strength.

To the woman who showed up
even when she was exhausted.
To the one who spoke out
even when her voice trembled.
To the ones who care, burn out,
and still find their way back to compassion.

Let these pages remind you:
Resilience is not toughness.
It is tenderness that has survived.

Burnout

When the Flame Flickers

Burnout doesn't always arrive with thunder. Sometimes, it seeps in like fog—slow, quiet, disorienting. You forget how to breathe properly. You're surrounded by people but feel alone. You stand in a beautiful place... and can't feel any of it.

I know this terrain well. I've walked it more than once. Over the years, I've met burnout in many forms. The overachiever who kept going long after her tank was empty. The caregiver who forgot she had needs of her own. The professional woman who smiled in every meeting, even as her spirit dimmed behind the smile.

And I'll be honest: I thought I should know better. After all, I'd studied burnout. Taught workshops on it. Built wellness programs around it. But insight alone doesn't shield us from the world's demands—or from the internal stories that drive us to keep going.

Even with the right habits in place—nourishment, movement, rest, meditation—there came a time when I simply... couldn't. My body said no. It took nearly a year to fully recover. And for a long time, I carried shame about that.

Until I realized: *Burnout wasn't a failure—it was a warning before something worse could take root.* My collapse was not weakness. It was wisdom. Because here's the truth: Burnout is not proof that you're not strong enough, balanced enough, grateful enough. It's often a sign that you've been *too* strong, *too* adaptable, in conditions no one was meant to endure forever. In a world that celebrates output and praises self-sacrifice, burnout is often the soul's final way of asking: *Will you come back to me?*

And now, it's not just personal—it's everywhere. Burnout has become cultural. Systemic. A quiet epidemic of women holding too much for too long: caregiving, uncertainty, emotional labour, digital noise, global grief. We are not breaking because we are weak. We are burning because we are lit from every angle—and no one ever taught us how to rest in the dark.

So, let these next few pages be a room. Not a lesson plan. Not a fix. Just a place to exhale. A place to be. A place to remember that you still exist beneath everything you do.

You'll find—

A curated list of Book Friends—stories that companion you gently back to yourself when the world feels too sharp.

A collection of whimsical, wonder-filled novels—perfect for disappearing into something softer, stranger, or simply more magical for a little while.

And if what you need right now is comfort more than clarity, or beauty without the burden of becoming—you'll find more offerings under *Fiction as Refuge* in the earlier *Stories as Sanctuary* section.

Let it all meet you where you are. Not where you're trying to be. Not where the world expects you to land. Just... here. In this breath. In this moment that doesn't need to be fixed or earned. And if all you do is rest in the softness of story, that is not avoidance. It is medicine. It is restoration.

May this be the beginning of something quieter. Not a comeback or reinvention. Just a return—gently—to yourself. Because even a flickering flame still carries light. And so do you.

Book Friends

These novels offer different textures of rebirth—from numbness and burnout to companionship and purpose. They don't rush healing. They simply sit with you, reminding you that feeling lost is part of the journey home.

My Year of Rest and Relaxation by Ottessa Moshfegh

Burned out by the world's absurdity and her own unprocessed grief, a young woman attempts to medicate herself into oblivion—

seeking peace not through healing but through disappearance. Set in early 2000s New York, this dark, sharp novel explores the emotional numbness that often follows burnout, and what's left when you try to sleep through your pain.

> *Why it helps:* Because it names the numbness many are afraid to admit. This novel gives voice to the darker impulse to disappear—and gently exposes what remains underneath.

The Party Crasher by Sophie Cousens

Effie, reeling from a recent breakup and a fractured family dynamic, finds herself sneaking into her dad's engagement party to retrieve a sentimental item—but she ends up eavesdropping on the life she's stepped away from. This lighthearted, big-hearted novel uses humour and chaos to explore how burnout often masks deeper hurt—and how joy and honesty can be found in the unlikeliest of places.

> *Why it helps:* Because laughter can be medicine. This novel gently reminds us that it's okay to be messy, to hide, and to come back out when you're ready, with humour and grace.

The Burnout by Sophie Kinsella

When Sasha finds herself utterly depleted by her high-pressure job and disconnected from her sense of purpose, she retreats to a seaside town for what she hopes will be a quiet escape. Instead, she meets Finn, a man also seeking solace. Their tentative connection becomes a shared path toward softness, honesty, and the rediscovery of joy.

Why it helps: Because it offers rest without shame. This story reminds us that slowing down, saying no, and starting fresh is not weakness; it's wisdom.

Hotel Silence by Auður Ava Ólafsdóttir

Jónas, a middle-aged man adrift in despair, travels to a war-torn country with a toolbox and a plan to end his life. Instead, he finds himself repairing not just broken buildings but also fractured lives—and, unknowingly, his own. This quiet, luminous novel explores how acts of service and unexpected connection can slowly rekindle a sense of purpose.

Why it helps: Because it reveals how repair begins with presence. This novel affirms that showing up—however quietly—can be the first act of healing.

What Are You Going Through by Sigrid Nunez

In this introspective novel, an unnamed narrator supports a terminally ill friend through her final days. Through their journey, the story delves into themes of compassion, mortality, and the complexities of human connection. Nunez's prose offers a contemplative look at how we navigate the emotional landscapes of others while confronting our own vulnerabilities.

Why it helps: Because it speaks to the quiet dignity of care. This story invites us to witness grief, love, and presence, all without rushing to fix a thing.

Magical Reprieve

For enchantment, delight, and the kind of healing that doesn't demand anything of you These are not books that ask you to grow. They simply invite you in. To laugh. To wonder.

To remember magic. To rest in a world that asks nothing but your willingness to enter.

The Lion, the Witch and the Wardrobe by C.S. Lewis
A snowy forest. A lamppost. A wardrobe that opens not just to another world but to the child within. This beloved first book in *The Chronicles of Narnia* series offers a tale of sacrifice, redemption, and wonder.

> ***Best for:*** Quiet afternoons, rekindling faith in goodness, or remembering that magic often hides in plain sight.

The Book Charmer by Karen Hawkins
In the small town of Dove Pond, books whisper to librarian Sarah Dove—and when newcomer Grace arrives with emotional baggage and her troubled niece, the books know she's the one who might save the town.

> ***Best for:*** Tender reawakenings, readers who believe books are alive, or when your heart needs a hopeful nudge.

The School for Good and Evil Series by Soman Chainani
This playful and sharp fantasy series flips the fairy-tale script. Two girls are whisked into opposing magical schools—one for good, one for evil—but nothing is as it seems. Full of humour, surprises, and twists on archetypes.

> ***Best for:*** Playful escapism, and girls who once loved fairy tales but now write their own endings.

The Ten Thousand Doors of January **by Alix E. Harrow**
In a sprawling mansion filled with artifacts, January Scaller discovers a strange book—one that reveals hidden doors to other worlds, and to the truth of her own history. Blending portal fantasy, lyrical prose, and themes of belonging, this novel is a love letter to stories as thresholds for transformation.

> *Best for:* When you crave a door out of the ordinary. For the woman who feels caught between chapters, this novel offers wonder, reclamation, and the quiet reminder that sometimes, the right story *is* the way through.

The Dallergut Dream Department Store **by Miye Lee**
In a whimsical, otherworldly town that exists only in dreams, there's a department store that sells sleep's most extraordinary offerings—adventures, nostalgia, peace, even courage. This novel offers a gentle, imaginative escape into the subconscious world of night.

> *Best for:* When waking life feels too loud. This novel is a soft exhale—a bedtime story for the soul, reminding us that wonder is a kind of medicine. Ideal for those longing to rest, to believe in quiet magic again, or to reconnect with the unseen inner lives we tend to in sleep.

Resilience

Stories That Strengthen Us

Resilience isn't loud. It doesn't always come with battle cries or bold declarations. Sometimes, it looks like getting up—again—after being knocked down by life's quiet devastations. Sometimes, it's holding your dignity in a room where it isn't mirrored back to you. Sometimes, it's choosing tenderness not because the world has been gentle, but because you refuse to let it harden you.

We often celebrate resilience in its most visible forms—achievements, recoveries, comebacks. But fiction shows us something deeper: the invisible resilience. The kind that lives in women who keep showing up. Who endure losses, betrayals, illnesses, silences—and still reach for beauty. Still cook dinner. Still raise children. Still whisper poems to themselves before bed.

Fiction gives us emotional companions—characters who survive what we've survived, or what we fear we might one day have to. These stories don't rush to solutions. They sit beside sorrow. They let characters fall apart before they rise. And in doing so, they give us permission to unfold in the same way.

Resilience is not just the ability to endure. It's the capacity to begin again, even after your voice has cracked, your hope has thinned, and your sense of direction has disappeared.

And perhaps most importantly, resilience is not a solo act. It's not heroic isolation. It's the quiet strength built over time, shaped by community, supported by memory, nourished by meaning.

Reading stories of resilience is not an escape. It's a form of gathering—a gathering of courage, of perspective, of the quiet knowing that you are not alone. That others have walked this road—barefoot, broken-hearted—and still made it home.

Book Friends
The Island of Sea Women **by Lisa See**
Set on the Korean island of Jeju, this powerful novel explores the decades-long friendship between two women who are part of a matrifocal diving collective. Amid war, betrayal, and generational pain, it reveals how resilience is shaped underwater, in silence, and through sisterhood.

> *Why it helps:* Because it honours strength that is neither loud nor celebrated. This story reminds us that resilience can be built in breath, in bond, and in the choices we make beneath the surface.

What Strange Paradise **by Omar El Akkad**
A haunting yet compassionate story of a young Syrian refugee boy washed ashore and the local girl who helps him survive. Told through dual timelines, this novel tenderly exposes the human face of migration and the instinct to protect, even in impossible circumstances.

> *Why it helps:* Because it shows that even in chaos, kindness endures. This novel restores our faith in small acts of courage, especially when the world turns away.

The Street of a Thousand Blossoms **by Gail Tsukiyama**
Set in Japan before, during, and after World War II, this sweeping novel follows two brothers whose lives are shaped by loss and discipline in the form of sumo wrestling and Noh mask carving. Through the women in their lives, we witness survival through war, widowhood, and quiet sacrifice.

> ***Why it helps:*** Because it reveals the many forms resilience can take: art, endurance, silence, and legacy. A quiet tribute to generational strength, especially in women.

The Lord of the Rings by J.R.R. Tolkien

An epic quest that spans realms, species, and the darkest parts of the self. At its core, this trilogy is not just about war or fantasy—but about the resilience of the ordinary, the sacred power of friendship, and the quiet heroism of those who never wanted greatness but rose to meet it.

> ***Why it helps:*** Because it shows that resilience is often not bold, but burdensome—and that the smallest among us may carry the heaviest loads with the most grace.

The Sound of Gravel by Ruth Wariner
(memoir that reads like fiction)

Born into a polygamist community in rural Mexico, Ruth Wariner's coming-of-age story is marked by poverty, abuse, and profound loss. And yet, through it all, she finds her way to education, autonomy, and safety—for herself and her siblings. Though a memoir, it reads with the intimacy and intensity of fiction.

> ***Why it helps:*** Because it shows that resilience can begin in childhood—quietly, in secret, in stolen moments of dreaming. Ruth's story reminds us that even in the darkest places, the instinct to protect, hope, and eventually rise is a force stronger than circumstance.

She Didn't Break

She didn't break—
though the world
tried to bend her
into silence.

She carried sorrow
the way others carry
shopping bags,
babies,
guilt.

But she still opened windows.
Still lit candles.
Still made soup
on the days when
grief sat beside her
like an old friend.

No one saw
how many times
she unraveled—
only how beautifully
she wove herself back together.

This is what they never say
about resilience:
It's not the absence of breaking.
It's the devotion to rising—
with strength, and courage,
again and again.

Chronic Illness & Disability

More than the Diagnosis

This chapter begins with someone I love. She has lived in pain every day for many years. A rare and excruciating condition was triggered after a routine surgery. Nothing about her pain is visible. But it is constant. It has changed the shape of her life.

She is beautiful. Brilliant. Sensitive. Strong. She had dreams—of a career, a family, a future. And while her peers were building those things, she was trying to stay upright in a world that does not understand what it means to hurt all the time.

What breaks my heart most isn't just what she has endured—it's how often people minimize it. Dismiss it. Treat her like she's exaggerating or just not trying hard enough. They walk ahead of her without looking back. They sigh at the wait. They fall silent in the face of her struggle, as if her pain is an inconvenience. As if her body's betrayal is a moral failing. As if needing compassion makes her difficult to love.

And yet—she hopes. She smiles. She asks how I'm doing. Her grace humbles me.

But it's not just hope she carries. It's discipline. Endurance. The quiet, daily work of someone who refuses to give up on her life. She reads. She questions. She advocates. She listens to her body, even when it screams. She tracks her symptoms, meditates, journals, paces herself. She tries, again and again, even when nothing gets better. She works harder to heal than most people work at anything. And still, she is doubted, dismissed, and left to explain a reality she never chose to carry. That, too, breaks me. And that, too, makes her extraordinary.

This chapter is for her. And for every person like her—especially women—who is surviving something no one else can see.

Because chronic illness and disability don't always come with wheelchairs or visible signs. Sometimes, they exist in bodies that appear "fine" but feel like fire. Sometimes, they wear a smile that hides the weight of simply getting through the day. Sometimes, they come wrapped not only in pain but in shame—not because of the condition itself, but because of the disbelief and discomfort it so often invites.

This section is not about overcoming. It is about witnessing. It is about honouring bodies that do not perform, that do not "bounce back," that do not fit cultural narratives of strength—but are strong anyway.

It is for the woman who has spent hours at appointments only to leave with more questions than answers. For the woman who avoids events, not because she doesn't care but because her body says no. For the woman whose worth is not in what she produces but in how she persists. It is for the woman who has redefined beauty, ambition, and meaning on her own terms. Who does not want to be seen as inspirational—just seen.

If that's you, this chapter is not here to fix anything. It is here to honour you. To say—

- **You are not weak**
- **You are not broken**
- **You are living in a body** that demands more from you than most people can imagine

And still – **you rise**

Book Friends

These stories don't centre on illness—they centre on humanity. Each one carries the quiet truth of what it means to live in a body that doesn't follow the rules. Tender, complex, and deeply relatable, these novels offer companionship more than cure.

All's Well by Mona Awad

Miranda is a theater professor battling relentless pain—and the dismissive doctors and colleagues who no longer believe her. Laced with dark humor and surreal twists, this novel explores what happens when a woman's suffering is ignored for too long and she reclaims power in unexpected, unnerving ways.

> ***Why it helps:*** Because it tells the truth about being disbelieved. This story honours the rage, grief, and magic of taking back your voice when no one is listening.

Get a Life, Chloe Brown by Talia Hibbert
A smart, funny romance with a heroine who lives with chronic pain—and decides to reclaim her joy, desire, and boldness one bucket-list item at a time. Warm, real, and refreshingly honest about invisible illness.

> ***Why it helps:*** Because it's radiant with possibility. Chloe reminds us that illness doesn't cancel pleasure, intimacy, or ambition; it just asks for a different rhythm.

Two Girls Staring at the Ceiling by Lucy Frank
Told in verse, this YA novel captures two teenagers sharing a hospital room, bonded by Crohn's disease and the unspoken fears of living in unpredictable bodies. Quietly powerful and full of emotional truth.

> ***Why it helps:*** Because it brings quiet fears into the light. This novel validates the loneliness and quiet bravery of young people navigating illness without easy answers.

The Fault in Our Stars by John Green
A story of love, mortality, and the search for meaning, told through the voice of a teenage girl living with cancer. Tender, funny, and deeply aware of the ache of being young in a body that is failing.

> *Why it helps:* Because it meets grief with grace. This story doesn't flinch from what hurts, but it still finds beauty in love, in laughter, and in the now.

Five Feet Apart by **Rachael Lippincott**

Two teens with cystic fibrosis fall in love—but they must remain physically apart due to health risks. A poignant portrait of intimacy, risk, and the yearning for connection when illness defines your world.

> *Why it helps:* Because it names the ache of longing. This novel honours the deep human need to connect—even when touch is impossible.

Blame by **Michelle Huneven**

A layered and reflective novel that follows Patsy MacLemoore, a history professor who, after a tragic accident and time in prison, must rebuild her life. While not centred on illness from the start, the second half of the novel deals directly with her experience of multiple sclerosis—its onset, progression, and quiet impact on identity, agency, and relationship.

> *Why it helps:* Because it portrays chronic illness not as the plot—but as a reality that changes everything, slowly and profoundly. With compassion and literary restraint, Huneven shows how illness reshapes ambition, self-perception, and love—not in melodrama, but in the stillness of living. A quiet, powerful witness to the complexity of endurance.

The Body Keeps the Score by Bessel van der Kolk *(nonfiction)*

This groundbreaking work on trauma and the nervous system offers both research and real-life insight into how bodies remember pain—often long after minds try to forget. Validating and empowering.

> *Why it helps:* Because it explains what many of us feel but can't articulate. This book bridges science and soul, showing that your body's responses are not weakness, but wisdom.

Between Two Kingdoms by Suleika Jaouad *(nonfiction)*

At 22, Jaouad was diagnosed with leukemia and spent years fighting for her life—only to discover that survival was its own kind of wilderness. This luminous memoir explores illness, identity, and the uncertain space between sickness and healing.

> *Why it helps:* Because it honours the after. This book walks with you not just through crisis but into the complicated quiet of survival and rebuilding.

She Carried It Quietly

She carried it quietly—
the pain, the fatigue, the fear
that her body might betray her
at any moment.

She showed up anyway.
Not always with strength,
but always with courage.

The world did not make space,
so she carved it.

With every breath,
every "I'm fine" that wasn't,
every step she took when rest
would've been easier,
she became a quiet monument
to endurance.

Not the kind that roars—
the kind that remains.

Climate Grief

To Grieve a Living World

There is a kind of grief many of us carry that has no funeral, no language, no clear beginning. It is the grief we feel for the planet—for forests lost, species gone, waters poisoned, air thickened, and futures dimmed. It is not a grief for something in the past. It is grief for what is vanishing even as we live it.

This grief can be quiet. Unseen. It rises in the grocery store when we notice all the plastic. In the anxiety that curls around weather alerts. In the helplessness we feel when watching wildfires consume communities—or when we wonder what kind of world we're leaving for the next generation. And because it feels too big to hold, too constant to soothe, we often bury it. But fiction makes it bearable.

Stories help us name what is otherwise invisible. They let us sit inside a disappearing forest and feel its voice. They allow us to grieve not in panic but in reverence. And reverence, in its quiet way, invites action.

As author Peter Wohlleben reminds us in *The Hidden Life of Trees*, forests are not just background—they are communities. Trees care for one another. They warn each other of danger. They nourish the sick and shelter the young. And in many old-growth forests, the oldest trees are like grandmothers—quietly sustaining those around them through unseen networks of root and mycorrhizal wisdom.

To grieve the earth is not just to weep for beauty lost. It is to mourn family. To mourn wisdom. To mourn kin.

This section is not about despair. It is about *remembering our belonging*. To the land. To each other. To the future we still have a chance to shape.

Fiction can be a bridge between knowing and caring. Between grief and responsibility. Between collapse and reimagining. Here are stories that help us hold that bridge.

Book Friends
Greenwood **by Michael Christie**
Spanning generations and told through a reverse timeline, this Canadian novel begins in a future where trees are scarce and precious. It then traces the roots—literal and metaphorical—of one family whose fate is inextricably linked to the forests of British Columbia.

> *Why it helps:* Because it mourns and marvels in the same breath. *Greenwood* explores environmental collapse without losing sight of beauty, connection, and legacy.

Flight Behavior **by Barbara Kingsolver**
In a rural Appalachian town, a woman discovers monarch butterflies behaving strangely—an ecological mystery that becomes a mirror for climate change and spiritual awakening.

> *Why it helps:* Because it translates global crisis into intimate experience, showing how awakening to nature can also awaken self-awareness, courage, and responsibility.

The Ministry for the Future **by Kim Stanley Robinson**
A sweeping speculative novel that imagines a future shaped by climate crisis and bold international action. Both terrifying and deeply hopeful.

> *Why it helps:* Because it refuses despair. It imagines solutions at scale—and asks what might be possible if we choose collective will over collapse.

Migrations by Charlotte McConaghy

A haunting tale of a woman tracking the last Arctic terns across a dying world. Lyrical and fierce, it asks how we live—and love—when extinction surrounds us.

> *Why it helps:* Because it makes ecological loss personal. It lets us grieve the vanishing while reminding us that even amid collapse, love—and purpose—can still rise.

Once There Were Wolves by Charlotte McConaghy

Set in the Scottish Highlands, this novel blends ecological restoration with personal healing as a biologist fights to reintroduce wolves to land—and to herself.

> *Why it helps:* Because it shows that restoration isn't just for the land—it's for the soul. And that rewilding the world begins with rewilding our inner lives.

The Hidden Life of Trees by Peter Wohlleben *(nonfiction)*

A quietly revolutionary book that reveals how trees communicate, support one another, and form vast underground networks of care.

> *Why it helps:* Because it shifts how we see forests—from scenery to community—and invites us to live with more reverence, reciprocity, and awe.

She Wept for the Earth and Was Not Alone

She didn't cry for herself,
not this time.

She cried for the river
that ran dry.
For the tree that stood for centuries
only to fall in silence.
For the bees that didn't return.
She cried not in panic—
but in reverence.

She touched a leaf as if it were skin.
She whispered "thank you"
to a crow overhead.

She stood barefoot,
not to ground, but to remember
she had roots too.

They told her she was too sensitive.
Too emotional. Too much.

But the soil heard her sorrow,
and the sky held her breath.

And the sea,
though far way
rolled one wave closer
in answer.

Fear, Collective Grief & World Trauma

When the World Feels Broken

There are days—too many lately—when it feels like the world is unraveling in real time.

You wake to headlines filled with war, injustice, collapse. You scroll through sorrow, rage, and helplessness, barely pausing to process before the next story breaks. The grief is constant. The fear, palpable. The nervous system, overwhelmed.

This is not history—it is now. And many of us are quietly breaking beneath its weight.

And yet, even in the midst of collective trauma, fiction gives us a lifeline. It doesn't erase reality—it helps us bear it. It slows the flood of information into something human. It shows us the people *inside* the headlines—their stories, their heartbreak, their hope.

In those moments, history books give us facts. But fiction gives us feeling. Fiction draws us close to the heartbeat of history. It doesn't just tell us what happened. It shows us who lived through it. Who loved through it. Who broke, and survived, and carried the echo of it in their bones.

To read *The Kite Runner* is to feel the unbearable weight of betrayal and the ache of redemption across decades and borders.

To read *Pachinko* is to witness the quiet endurance of a family cast across generations of exile, prejudice, and impossible choices—where history's brutality lives not only in war but in the quiet ache of displacement.

To read *All the Light We Cannot See* is to walk through occupied France with eyes wide open to both beauty and ruin.

In fractured times—then and now—fiction restores dimension to what might otherwise be flattened by distance or data. It refuses to let us look away. It makes us feel what the numbers cannot. And in doing so, it calls us to care.

Stories like these are not passive. They are not neutral. They are witnesses. They speak when silence becomes dangerous. They awaken empathy when indifference threatens to numb us.

And when the world feels unrecognizable, stories help us remember what is essential:

That others have survived times like this. That courage is often quiet. That resilience is often ordinary. That hope, somehow, still rises.

We read not to escape history but to carry its wisdom forward. To name what hurts. To honour what matters. To become, in our own quiet way, part of the remembering.

Book Friends

These novels span continents, centuries, and conflicts, but all share one thing in common: they help us feel history. Each one offers a window into what it means to live through upheaval, loss, resilience, and transformation. These are not just books—they are emotional time machines.

Nigeria:
Half of a Yellow Sun by Chimamanda Ngozi Adichie

Set during the Biafran War in Nigeria, this powerful novel explores the emotional toll of civil war through love, identity, and loss.

> *Why it helps:* Because it makes visible the human cost of political conflict—and honours the stories of those history often erases.

Ghana:
Homegoing by Yaa Gyasi

A multigenerational saga following two Ghanaian half-sisters and the ripple of slavery through their descendants across centuries and continents.

> *Why it helps:* Because it maps inherited trauma with deep compassion, and shows that the past is not behind us, but within us.

Vietnam:
The Mountains Sing by Nguy n Phan Qu Mai
Spanning the Vietnam War and its aftermath, this novel offers a deeply personal lens on survival, culture, and family resilience.

> *Why it helps:* Because it places a mother and daughter's voice at the center of a war narrative, reminding us that endurance is often feminine—and fierce.

Palestine:
Salt Houses by Hala Alyan
Follows four generations of a Palestinian family navigating displacement, identity, and the lingering grief of exile.

> *Why it helps:* Because it gives voice to what is often left unsaid—how loss travels across generations, and how home becomes both place and longing.

India:
A Fine Balance by Rohinton Mistry
Set during India's Emergency in the 1970s, this sweeping novel follows four strangers who form an unlikely bond amid political upheaval, poverty, and loss.

> *Why it helps:* Because it holds both suffering and tenderness in the same breath, reminding us that humanity endures even when hope feels thin.

Afghanistan:
The Kite Runner **by Khaled Hosseini**
A powerful tale of friendship, betrayal, and redemption set against the backdrop of Afghanistan's shifting political landscape.

> *Why it helps:* Because it speaks to the ache of guilt, the cost of silence, and the redemptive power of returning—no matter how long it takes.

Germany:
All the Light We Cannot See **by Anthony Doerr**
A lyrical, deeply humane story of a blind French girl and a German soldier during WWII, showing the persistence of beauty and connection amid ruin.

> *Why it helps:* Because it reminds us that light still moves through rubble—and that even in wartime, tenderness finds a way.

Korea/Japan:
Pachinko **by Min Jin Lee**
A sweeping multigenerational saga following a Korean family exiled to Japan during the early 20th century. *Pachinko* explores how history inscribes itself onto ordinary lives—and how women, in particular, carry that legacy with grace and grit.

> *Why it helps:* This novel makes history personal. Through its immersive storytelling and emotional clarity, *Pachinko* offers readers a way to feel the weight of generational trauma and cultural displacement—without being overwhelmed or distanced from the emotional truth.

Bosnia:
The Cellist of Sarajevo by **Steven Galloway**
Set during the Siege of Sarajevo, this novel follows four civilians trying to survive in a city torn apart by war, while a lone cellist plays music in defiance of violence.

> ***Why it helps:*** Because it reminds us that art can be a form of resistance—and that even in the face of atrocity, humanity and grace can still rise.

Chile:
A Long Petal of the Sea by **Isabel Allende**
Follows two Spanish Civil War refugees who flee to Chile and navigate decades of political unrest, exile, and love in their adopted homeland.

> ***Why it helps:*** Because it shows that the journey of healing is rarely linear—and that exile, love, and memory often live in the same heart.

What Fiction Remembers

When the history books grow quiet,
fiction keeps whispering.

It remembers the mother who waited,
the child who fled,
the soldier who broke,
the lover who stayed behind.

It carries the ache of exile,
the breathless hush before the siren,
the hunger that had no name.

We do not just read these stories.
We enter them—
walk their rubble-lined streets,
sleep in their shadows,
wake with their questions.

And in doing so,
we become witnesses too.

Because fiction does not flinch.
It remembers what the world
tries to forget.

Staying Human in a Cruel World

Feeling Without Falling Apart

Some mornings, the news feels like a slow unraveling of everything sacred. The images come too fast. A child in rubble. A mother screaming. A place that once had music—now dust. It feels unthinkable. And yet, it keeps happening. Genocide. Ethnic cleansing. Babies erased. Women dehumanized. Entire communities flattened by bombs while the world debates their worthiness.

Not just loss—but cruelty. Not just grief—but brutality so sharp it leaves an imprint on your nervous system. You see the images. You hear the cries. You scroll past headlines you can't unsee.

And if you feel like you're carrying too much—you are. Because you care. And that caring, if left unguarded, can turn into sorrow without end.

This section is not about grief for what's lost. It's about surviving the *knowing*. About feeling everything—but not letting it hollow you out.

If you feel helpless in the face of it, you're not broken. **You're awake.** And being awake in this world is not easy. But it is necessary.

This section is for those who feel it all. Who carry both heartbreak and horror. Who don't want to shut down but also don't want to collapse. It's for the sensitive ones—the feelers, the watchers, the quiet noticers of pain.

It's not weakness to feel. It's not overreaction to care. But empathy, unguarded, becomes erosion. Compassion without boundaries can turn into burnout, despair, or complicity. And sensitivity, without tools, becomes suffering.

To keep feeling in a cruel world, you must also know when to step back and ask: *How do I stay present without being consumed?*

How do I keep my heart open without letting it be broken again and again?

These stories will not absolve cruelty. They will not excuse what must be condemned. But they will help you understand how people become capable of harm—not to justify, but to see clearly. Because cruelty is not always born of evil. Sometimes, it's born of indoctrination, of fear, or of unhealed trauma passed down like inheritance.

Understanding cruelty allows us to stop absorbing it. To witness it without letting it define us. To stay human in the face of inhumanity.

You do not have to carry what history keeps repeating. **You do not have to harden to survive.**

Let these stories walk beside you as you reclaim your clarity. The kind that stays rooted in love but protected by discernment. The kind that says: *"I see you. But I will not bleed for you."*

Book Friends

Stories that explore how cruelty is formed—not to excuse it, but to understand the wounds behind it

The Reader by Bernhard Schlink

Set in post-WWII Germany, this novel explores the relationship between a teenager and an older woman, who is later revealed to have been a concentration camp guard.

> *Why it helps:* A deeply human story about guilt, ignorance, and complicity. It shows how shame and silence can shape a person's capacity for harm—and how understanding can exist without absolution.

Disgrace by J.M. Coetzee

A professor in South Africa faces disgrace after inappropriate conduct, then retreats to his daughter's farm—where violence and power unfold in unexpected ways.

> ***Why it helps:*** This novel reveals how cultural trauma, ego, and unhealed wounds perpetuate cruelty. It doesn't excuse behavior, but rather invites reflection on what shapes it.

The Dinner by Herman Koch

Two couples meet at a restaurant to discuss a disturbing crime their sons have committed, revealing uncomfortable truths about morality and protection.

> ***Why it helps:*** This unsettling story examines how people justify harm to maintain comfort, control, or appearances. It offers sharp insight into moral dissonance and quiet complicity.

Lord of the Flies by William Golding

When a group of schoolboys is stranded on an island, they descend into savagery—revealing the fragility of civility.

> ***Why it helps:*** A stark portrayal of groupthink, fear, and the ease with which moral codes dissolve under pressure. It reminds us how quickly cruelty can become a collective language, and how fragile our civility truly is.

My Dark Vanessa by Kate Elizabeth Russell

A woman revisits her past relationship with a much older teacher who manipulated her as a teen, forcing her to re-examine what she once called love.

> ***Why it helps:*** Because it shows how power can wear the mask of affection—and how understanding the

psychology of harm includes confronting how easily it hides behind charisma, silence, or self-blame.

The Round House by Louise Erdrich

Set on an Ojibwe reservation, this novel follows a teenage boy seeking justice for his mother after she is brutally attacked. It explores generational trauma, legal injustice, and how violence weaves itself into identity and land.

> *Why it helps:* Because it sheds light on the quiet, ongoing cruelty of legal systems that fail Indigenous women and the ripple of grief and rage that emerges when justice is denied. A powerful, intimate portrait of harm, resilience, and sacred rage.

The Nickel Boys by Colson Whitehead

Based on the true story of a reform school in Jim Crow-era Florida, this novel follows two Black boys navigating violence, abuse, and survival inside a system that claims to "rehabilitate."

> *Why it helps:* Because it exposes how institutions disguise cruelty as discipline—and how racism, power, and silence shape the futures of those caught inside. A deeply haunting reminder that cruelty often hides behind structure and justification.

The Murmur of Bees by Sofía Segovia

Set during the Mexican Revolution and the 1918 influenza pandemic, this lush novel follows a mysterious, bee-covered child named Simonopio, found abandoned and believed to be blessed—or cursed. Taken in by a family on a rural hacienda, his quiet presence and mystical gifts shape their fate through decades of upheaval.

Why it helps: Because it weaves personal loss, political unrest, and ancestral knowing into a rich tapestry of love, land, and legacy. A magical meditation on how even in brutal times, beauty and belonging can endure—and sometimes, the quietest souls carry the greatest wisdom.

Collective Cruelty

Cruelty doesn't always wear a mask. Sometimes it stands at a podium. Sometimes it passes laws. Sometimes it goes viral.

Collective cruelty happens when a group—whether a schoolyard, a government, or a nation—learns to other, dehumanize, or punish under the guise of safety, tradition, or righteousness. It often begins in silence: when people look away, laugh nervously, or convince themselves that it's "not that bad."

But beneath every movement fueled by hate is something ancient: **fear.** Fear of losing power. Fear of being wrong. Fear of the unfamiliar, the vulnerable, or the truth.

We've seen it throughout history—in internment camps, in segregated schools, in banned books, in sterilization laws, in witch trials, in mobs.

And we're seeing it now.

The antidote is not more outrage. It's clarity. The kind that sees injustice, names it, and refuses to join the chorus of cruelty. The kind that walks with compassion but does not kneel to harm.

Because the soul of a culture is shaped by what it tolerates in public—and what it justifies in private.

The Cost of the Mask

They say they want freedom,
but mean dominion.
They cry for truth,
but flinch from their own.

So they drape themselves in flags,
chant louder than their grief,
and call kindness weakness—
because it reminds them
of all they were told not to feel.

Their anger is not new.
It is the child no one comforted.
It is the shame
no one helped them name.

And still—
they mock the hurting,
strike the soft,
and wear cruelty like armour.

But here is the cost:
you cannot be cruel
without slicing through your own soul.

And so the wound festers,
and so the hate grows,
and so they scream into the dark—
terrified that love
might show them who they've become.

To expand is to include
To include is to remember we belong to one another

Part V: Stories that Expand Us

There are stories that widen the lens –
that dismantle assumptions
and dissolve the distance
between self and other.

These stories move us
not because they are about us,
but because they remind us
that we are all connected.

Chapter 17: Stories that Expand Us

There are stories that hold us close—familiar, comforting, echoing truths we already carry. They offer resonance, safety, and reflection. And then there are the stories that do something else entirely. They don't just soothe us. They stretch us.

These are the stories that usher us toward the unknown, the misunderstood, the misrepresented. They invite us to leave the comfortable borders of our beliefs and inhabit another's truth—not as a tourist of suffering, not as a rescuer or a voyeur, but as a witness. As someone willing to feel what they feel, even when it's hard. Especially when it's hard.

This chapter is devoted to that kind of story. Not as an intellectual exercise—but as a spiritual, emotional, and ethical offering. Because true empathy begins not in agreement but in attention. In listening long enough for the surface to break. In feeling someone else's story in your own skin.

In a world obsessed with certainty and speed, fiction becomes the antidote. It slows us down. It dismantles the armor of assumption. It unhooks us from the reflex to judge and invites us instead to sit, still and open, in the living room of another's soul. These aren't just stories. They're expansions. They ask—

Can you see beyond your lens?

Can you sit in the fire of someone else's experience—without rushing to extinguish it?

Can you allow another life to reshape the architecture of your understanding?

This section is built around four doorways—each leading somewhere necessary:

Global Stories

Here we travel into landscapes far from our own—culturally, geographically, emotionally. These stories aren't postcards; they're immersion. They challenge the western gaze and ask us to see from within, not above. They say: *This is our home. Walk through it with care.* They don't just show us what's different. They illuminate what's shared. Grief. Hope. Kinship. Longing.

Stories of the Displaced

Migration. Exile. Asylum. These are not abstract policies—they are deeply human upheavals. And in fiction, the displaced are not statistics. They are fathers who can no longer sleep. Daughters who carry keys to houses they may never return to. Artists who paint in camps. Mothers who walk miles in silence so their children won't hear their fear. These stories give us back the faces that headlines erase. They do not plead. They testify. They remind us that home is not always a place—it is often a person, a memory, or a dream stitched inside a suitcase.

Lives Behind Bars—Incarcerated Women

This section gives voice to those whom society often forgets. Women who were once girls never believed. Women shaped by poverty, addiction, trauma—and whose stories were lost behind courtroom doors. In fiction, they become whole again. Their sentences do not define them; their stories do. We see the mother writing letters to a child she cannot hold. The survivor healing through poetry. The friend, the sister, the self—not erased, but revealed. These pages ask us to look deeper than a charge or a label. To see the humanity beneath the headline.

LGBTQ+ Lives

This section is not about proving worth—it is about honouring it. These stories carry the full range of life: love and rupture, silence and song, exile and arrival. They are not only about identity—they are about becoming. About claiming space where it was once denied. About choosing authenticity over approval.

Unity Within Diversity

In a world shaped by migration, displacement, and cultural evolution, many feel the ground shifting beneath them. Familiar ways of life begin to change. Languages, customs, even food traditions blend or vanish. And with this comes unease—a fear that identity may be diluted, and that what once felt like home is slowly being rewritten.

At the same time, those who arrive in new lands often carry their own silent grief: the ache of exile, the uncertainty of integration, the longing to be accepted without having to erase who they are.

What if this was not a rupture but a moment of possibility?

Fiction invites us to inhabit lives beyond our own borders. Through story, we can walk beside someone whose language we do not speak, whose god we do not worship, whose culture is not ours—and still recognize the humanness within them.

The stories in this section do not pretend that integration is easy. They do not romanticize displacement.

Instead, they offer emotional insight into the deep complexity of belonging—what it means to lose it, to find it again, or to create it anew.

Spirituality, when it rises beyond doctrine, reminds us that we are more than our origins. That our soul is not bound by geography. And that true belonging is not sameness—it is recognition.

We do not need to fear difference. We need only to meet it with reverence.

Chapter 18: Global Stories

Reading Across Cultures

I've had the extraordinary privilege of visiting more than 55 countries—most of them as a solo traveler. That's not a boast. It's a confession of gratitude and a recognition that travel, for me, has never been about escape or entertainment. It has been a form of education. A slow awakening.

Across deserts and coastlines, night markets and mountain villages, I have been welcomed, warned, humbled, and changed. I have sat with women in silence and laughter, in languages we didn't share but somehow still understood. I have listened to their stories and seen, again and again, how alike we are beneath the noise of difference.

We all want safety for our children. We all long to be seen without fear. We all carry grief. We all carry beauty.

And yet, I have also seen—and continue to see—too much cruelty. Some of it systemic. Some of it so normalized it barely registers. Much of it aimed at women and girls. And, too often, allowed to continue because it doesn't touch *us*.

But it does.

It touches us because we are one body, whether we admit it or not. When a child is pulled from their parent at a border, when a pregnant woman is left to give birth in a cell, when a young girl is silenced, sold, or shamed—we are diminished too. Not as women. As humans.

This section is not here to preach, or to scold, or to politicize. It's here to *expand*. To invite. To help us soften our edges and open our eyes. Because sometimes, what the news numbs, fiction awakens.

Stories from other cultures offer us more than awareness. They offer us kinship. They remind us that someone, somewhere, is living a life we've never imagined but may urgently need to understand.

And that maybe, in reading their story, we become better caretakers of our own.

Something shifts when we open a book from another world and realize it speaks to something within our own. Stories don't just cross borders—they cross into us.

Not all growth is loud. Sometimes, it happens quietly—in the space between a sentence and a sigh, when we find ourselves caring deeply for a character whose life looks nothing like our own.

This is the quiet power of fiction: It teaches us to feel with, not just think about. Empathy isn't just a trait. It's a muscle. And fiction—unlike almost any other medium—works it gently, deeply, over time.

When we step into someone else's shoes, even for a few pages, we're invited to practice something essential: emotional understanding. We begin to notice the subtleties of human behavior. We recognize pain before it's named. We become more comfortable sitting with discomfort—not rushing to fix, but learning how to witness.

Fiction gives us a window into lives we might never live. It invites us to walk for a while in someone else's skin—not as tourists, but as witnesses. Through the eyes of characters from different backgrounds, beliefs, or bodies, we begin to understand not just what they face but what they feel.

Emotional intelligence, too, is shaped by story. Characters who are flawed but learning. Dialogues that show what's left unsaid. Plotlines that force reflection on what matters most. These aren't just entertainment—they're training grounds for connection.

In a world that often rewards speed, certainty, and surface-level interaction, fiction invites us to slow down, listen closely, and soften. To become less reactive and more reflective. More nuanced in our judgments. More spacious in our hearts. And perhaps most importantly, more able to recognize our shared humanity—even when it looks unfamiliar.

This section is dedicated to stories that stretch us, that reach across divides, that soften judgment. That challenge stereotypes and invite a deeper seeing. Not every book will be easy. Some will unsettle; others will illuminate. But all will expand our capacity to connect.

Let this section offer stories that open—not with perfection, but with presence. Because emotional intelligence isn't about knowing more. It's about feeling wisely. And empathy begins exactly where story begins: with attention. With curiosity. With care.

Book Friends
These books take us to places our passports never could but where our hearts always needed to go.

India:
The Henna Artist by Alka Joshi
Set in 1950s Jaipur, this novel immerses readers in the cultural and societal constraints faced by women carving out independent lives.

> *Why it helps:* Because it centers on a woman claiming her autonomy in a world that demands conformity—and shows how artistry can become both refuge and resistance.

Cameroon/United States:
Behold the Dreamers by Imbolo Mbue
Follows a Cameroonian immigrant family striving for stability in post-9/11 New York during the financial collapse.

> *Why it helps:* Because it brings empathy to the immigrant experience, making visible the dreams, fears, and dignity behind headlines and policy debates.

Japan:
Kitchen by Banana Yoshimoto
Set in Tokyo, this novella captures loneliness, gender identity, and quiet resilience in contemporary Japanese life.

> *Why it helps:* This story invites us into intimate emotional spaces where love and loss coexist, and where solitude is not loneliness but transformation.

Afghanistan:
A Thousand Splendid Suns by Khaled Hosseini
Spanning thirty years of Afghan history, this novel follows two women—Mariam and Laila—whose lives become intertwined through marriage, war, and survival in a society that often denies them voice and agency.

> *Why it helps:* Because it offers a deeply compassionate view into the inner lives of women living through political oppression and cultural constraint, reminding us that resilience can be born in even the harshest conditions and that love, though fragile, endures.

Nigeria:
Girl by Edna O'Brien
A haunting novel inspired by the real-life abduction of Nigerian schoolgirls by Boko Haram, this story follows one girl's journey through captivity, loss, and the long road back to self.

> *Why it helps:* Explores trauma, violation, and survival through a fictional lens rooted in real-world truth. This novel offers witness to the emotional

aftermath of coercion and the quiet courage required to reclaim identity. For readers who have endured betrayal, displacement, or erasure, *Girl* offers a deeply human reminder: You are not alone, and you are not broken.

United States:
An American Marriage by Tayari Jones

Set in the contemporary American South, this novel explores the emotional toll of wrongful incarceration on a Black couple navigating love, justice, and identity.

> ***Why it helps:*** Because it shows how systems can shape—and strain—intimate lives, while reminding us that love is rarely simple but always worthy of deeper seeing.

Where the Heart Widens

Not all revolutions arrive with noise.
Some begin in silence—
in the moment you pause
to a sentence that startles you
with its tenderness.

You didn't think you'd care for her.
But now you do.
You didn't think you'd understand him.
But somehow you do.

Fiction has no agenda
but to make you feel.
And in feeling,
you begin to stretch—
beyond your judgments,
beyond your certainty,
beyond your skin.

This is how the heart widens.
Not through argument,
but through story.
The right novel doesn't just entertain.
It rearranges you.

Chapter 19: Stories of the Displaced

Fiction that Opens the Heart

A cross borders, oceans, deserts, and invisible lines, millions of lives are uprooted every year—not by choice, but by violence, poverty, persecution, and fear. These are not crises of movement. They are crises of *belonging*.

To be displaced is to lose more than geography. It is to lose safety. To lose certainty. To lose the quiet dignity of being seen as fully human.

And yet, what is often lost in the headlines—what is flattened by politics and fear—is the emotional truth of these lives. Their longing. Their love. Their courage. Their complexity.

These stories ask us to remember that no one flees home unless home has become unlivable. That people do not risk everything—children in arms, oceans beneath them—for adventure or advantage. They do it for survival. For their families. For a sliver of hope.

Fiction offers what policy rarely can: a way in.

A way to walk beside those we've been taught to fear or forget. A way to remember that borders may define countries—but they do not define worth.

The novels in this section are not designed to comfort. They are here to soften the places that have gone numb. To pierce the noise of division with stories that ask, quietly but firmly: *"What if this were your family? Your home? Your child?"*

Because when we listen—truly listen—to the stories of the displaced, we begin to loosen the borders around our own hearts.

We begin to remember that no human is illegal. That empathy is not weakness. That to care is not naïve—it is courageous.

Book Friends
Exit West by Mohsin Hamid
In a nameless country on the brink of collapse, Saeed and Nadia fall in love—and flee through magic doors that transport them to distant places. A modern parable about migration, identity, and transformation.

> *Why it helps:* Because it reframes displacement not only as trauma but as transformation, asking us to imagine not just what is lost but what is still possible.

What Strange Paradise by Omar El Akkad
After a deadly boat crossing, a young Syrian boy washes up on an island and is found by a local girl. Their fragile bond is the heart of this urgent novel, which explores the refugee crisis through a child's eyes.

> *Why it helps:* Because it makes the unimaginable personal and asks us to witness the cost of our indifference with unflinching tenderness.

The Map of Salt and Stars by Zeyn Joukhadar
Blending myth and contemporary reality, this novel follows a Syrian girl fleeing civil war while echoing the journey of a 12th-century mapmaker.

> *Why it helps:* Because it reminds us that displacement is not new—and that story, even when fractured, can be a thread that ties us to identity, history, and survival.

The Same Sky by **Amanda Eyre Ward**
Told in alternating voices, this novel follows a teenager making a treacherous journey from Honduras to Texas, and a Texas woman navigating grief and infertility.

> *Why it helps:* Because it bridges worlds, showing how different forms of longing, loss, and love can ultimately connect us in unexpected ways.

American Dirt by **Jeanine Cummins**
Lydia, a bookstore owner in Acapulco, and her son Luca are forced to flee Mexico after a brutal act of cartel violence. Their journey north is harrowing, marked by danger, exhaustion, and moments of unexpected kindness.

> *Why it helps:* Because it gives a face—and a mother's heart—to the migrant experience, reminding us that no wall can silence the desperation of a parent trying to protect their child.

The Beekeeper of Aleppo by **Christy Lefteri**
Nuri and Afra, once gentle keepers of bees, become refugees after the war in Syria takes everything from them—including their son. Their story is one of memory, trauma, and the fragile hope that flickers even in ruin.

> *Why it helps:* Because it brings emotional depth to a global crisis, showing how love can endure even when everything familiar has been lost.

The Ones Who Walked

They did not leave
for pleasure,
for leisure,
for anything resembling ease.

They left
because the ground cracked open.
Because the air filled with smoke.
Because the silence at night
was no longer safe.

They walked
with babies strapped to backs,
with memories wrapped in cloth,
with names whispered like prayers
to keep them alive
on the other side.

They walked
toward fences,
toward oceans,
toward promises
made of headlines
and hope.

And the world looked away.

But not you.

You opened a page
and there they were—
not numbers,
not shadows,

but faces,
fathers,
mothers
daughters.

And in that moment,
your heart made room.
You did not fix.
You did not save.
You simply stayed—
and bore witness.

Because some journeys
do not need our judgment
They need our presence.

To walk beside someone,
even in story,
is to say:
You matter.
You belong.
You are no longer alone.

Returning to Empathy

What if the border was in us?

What if the divide we are meant to cross is not only between nations, but between fear and compassion?

It is easy to say, *not my problem*. It is easy to believe, *they are not like me*. But what if they are?

What if you had been born in another country, to different skies, different rules, different risks? What if the only thing separating your life from theirs was geography—and chance?

When we read the stories of the displaced, we are not just expanding our knowledge. We are reclaiming our *humanness*.

The next time someone speaks with cruelty—about migrants, about borders, about "others"—you don't need to argue. You don't need to shout.

But you can say, *"I've heard their stories. And once you've heard their stories—you can't uncare."*

Because empathy isn't an opinion.

It's a return.

To the kind of person you've always wanted to be.

Chapter 20: Incarcerated Women

Stories from the Inside: When Women Are Forgotten

I imagine this section may surprise you.

It surprised me, too.

It was born from a brief conversation with a friend—a passing remark, really—about a prison guard who had seen firsthand the difference a small prison library made in the lives of inmates. Curious, I began to look into it. What I found stopped me in my tracks.

In Canada, charitable organizations like the John Howard Society and Book Clubs for Inmates have stepped in to make sure books reach those who need them most—from legal resources to memoirs to literary fiction. And among them, it is often *fiction* that offers the deepest emotional refuge. Not escape, but entry. Not distraction, but depth. These programs don't just offer access; they offer dignity.

Most women in prison were once girls in pain—abused, abandoned, addicted, or simply poor. They are not a separate category of humanity. **They are us.** They are not gone. They are hidden—behind bars, behind shame, behind a society that rarely asks *what brought them there*. But when they are given the chance to write, speak, or simply be heard, what emerges is not criminality but clarity.

This section is for the women we overlook. The ones whose stories are so often silenced—by the justice system, by circumstance, and by public indifference. And it's also for the reader who may never step inside a prison but who can still step inside these pages with an open heart.

When I began writing *The Fiction Fix*, I knew that story had the power to soothe us after hard days. But I've come to realize it does something far greater: It sustains us through impossible ones.

For many incarcerated women, fiction becomes a form of survival. A mirror. A doorway. It comforts. It reflects. It teaches. And sometimes—miraculously—it frees. Not from the sentence, but from the belief that they are no longer human.

Including this section felt essential—not as a detour, but as a return. To what fiction does best: **meet people where they are and offer them back to themselves.**

Because if story can offer light in the darkest places, it can do the same for all of us.

Book Friends
The Mars Room by Rachel Kushner
A gripping literary novel centered on Romy, a woman sentenced to life in prison, as she navigates the dehumanizing world of the correctional system.

> *Why it helps:* Because it offers a visceral look at the emotional and psychological toll of incarceration. Reminds women of their worth, even when systems seek to erase it.

Affinity by Sarah Waters
Set in 1870s London, this gothic novel follows Margaret Prior, a woman who begins visiting a women's prison as part of her charitable work.

> *Why it helps:* Because it explores how emotional isolation, secrecy, and longing for connection unfold in confined spaces—both literal and emotional.

The Walls Around Us by Nova Ren Suma
This young adult novel intertwines the lives of three girls—two incarcerated in a juvenile detention center, and one a ballerina on the outside.

> *Why it helps:* Because it helps readers reflect on justice, redemption, and the complexity of becoming. Especially powerful for young women caught in cycles of harm, grief, or silence.

History of Ash by Khadija Marouazi
A Moroccan novel that follows Mouline and Leila, political prisoners during Morocco's Years of Lead.

> *Why it helps:* Because it illuminates the strength of women under authoritarian rule, and offers insight into emotional endurance, inner resistance, and spiritual survival.

Nonfiction Voices: Testimonies from Within
Prisoner of Tehran by Marina Nemat
At sixteen, Marina was arrested, tortured, and sentenced to death in Iran's notorious Evin Prison for speaking out against the regime.

> *Why it helps:* A memoir of wrongful imprisonment and survival, it reminds readers of the power of voice, even in silence.

Corrections in Ink by Keri Blakinger
A former figure skater turned addict, Blakinger shares her journey through prison and her return to self with fierce honesty.

> *Why it helps:* Because it affirms that healing is nonlinear—and that reclaiming one's voice is the deepest form of freedom.

Memoirs from the Women's Prison by Nawal El Saadawi
Written during her own incarceration, El Saadawi's account exposes political repression and solidarity behind bars.

> *Why it helps:* Because it offers truth without apology. For readers who've been silenced, this is both witness and mirror.

Inside This Place, Not of It by Ayelet Waldman & Robin Levi
Thirteen firsthand accounts from women incarcerated in the U.S., each revealing systemic abuse and enduring strength.

> *Why it helps:* Because it dismantles stereotypes and builds emotional bridges through truth-telling.

Couldn't Keep It to Myself by Wally Lamb & the Women of York Correctional Institution
A collection of autobiographical essays from incarcerated women in Connecticut.

> *Why it helps:* Because it reminds us that every story matters—and that writing is a reclamation of both self and truth.

The Ones We Erased

*What the Numbers Won't Say Aloud
(Canada & the U.S.A.)*

- In Canada, **over 40%** of federally incarcerated women are Indigenous—though they make up **less than 5%** of the general female population.

- In the U.S., **over 60%** of women in prison are mothers—many of them the sole caregivers.

- In Canada, the number of federally incarcerated women has increased by **more than 50%** over the past two decades—making them the fastest-growing prison population.

- In both countries, **most women are imprisoned for nonviolent offences**—often linked to poverty, addiction, trauma, or survival.

- Studies show that in Canada, **68%** of federally incarcerated women have experienced physical abuse, and **53%** have experienced sexual abuse.

- Across both nations, **many incarcerated women were victims long before they were ever labelled offenders.**

The Caged Still Sing

They took her name
and gave her a number.
Took her voice
and called it defiance.

Took her story and rewrote it in headlines
she never approved.

But they could not take
the song beneath her silence.

In the dark,
she remembered who she'd been—
before the hand, before the needle,
before the shame had a roof and a cell.

She braided poems into her pillow.
She whispered prayers through vents.
She stitched memory onto paper,
smuggling hope past the guards.

Her freedom did not wait for release.
It lived in every word
they told her not to write.
In every tear she was taught not to shed.
In every name
she dared to reclaim.

Because even caged,
she still sang.
And someone, somewhere,
finally listened.

Chapter 21: Seeing with New Eyes

Stories that Open the Door to LGBTQ+ Lives

It's hard to hate up close.
That's the quiet truth of story. When we read with care, we sit with people we've never met and feel what they feel. We begin to understand—not by argument, but by intimacy.

Queer lives have long been flattened into stereotypes or erased altogether. But fiction resists that flattening. It gives us characters who love bravely, suffer deeply, and carry questions about identity, family, belonging, and becoming—just like everyone else.

This section is not here to preach or persuade. It's here to **expand the emotional imagination**. To invite those who've been taught to fear LGBTQ+ people to *see them*, in all their nuance, humanity, and courage. Because the more we read, the harder it becomes to "other" someone, and the louder the call becomes not just for tolerance, but for tenderness.

Stories can't erase hatred. But they can interrupt it. They can slow it down. They can say, *"Look again. This is a life."* And that's where change begins.

Book Friends

These novels were chosen not just for representation but for their ability to open hearts. Each story invites readers into the emotional interior of queer lives—lives often misunderstood or maligned. These are not cautionary tales; they are windows, mirrors, and quiet revolutions.

***Giovanni's Room* by James Baldwin**
A young American man in 1950s Paris wrestles with love, shame, and identity in this searing, timeless classic.

> ***Why it helps:*** Because it exposes the raw ache of self-denial and the cost of a world that won't let love speak its name.

***The Black Flamingo* by Dean Atta**
Told in verse, this powerful YA novel follows a mixed-race gay teen in the UK as he discovers self-expression through drag and poetry.

> ***Why it helps:*** Because it celebrates queer joy and identity with boldness and grace, reminding us that self-love is its own revolution.

***The Great Believers* by Rebecca Makkai**
Spanning the AIDS crisis in 1980s Chicago and the long-reaching impact decades later, this novel weaves grief, friendship, and resilience into a powerful tapestry of human connection.

> ***Why it helps:*** Because it shows what happens when a society looks away—and what it means to love, lose, and still believe in beauty amid devastation.

***Juliet Takes a Breath* by Gabby Rivera**
When Juliet, a Puerto Rican queer teen from the Bronx, spends the summer interning with a white feminist author, her world cracks open in ways that challenge and liberate her.

Why it helps: Because it explores intersectionality with warmth, wit, and fierce clarity, reminding us that identity isn't just one thing, and liberation is deeply personal.

You Should See Me in a Crown by Leah Johnson

When Liz Lighty, a smart and ambitious Black teen, decides to run for prom queen to win a college scholarship, she doesn't expect to fall for the competition. Set in a small Midwestern town, this joyful YA novel celebrates first love, self-worth, and queer Black girl magic.

Why it helps: Because it centers queer joy. This is a story about belonging, bravery, and blooming in a world that tries to dim your light—and it reminds us that sometimes, being seen is the most radical thing of all.

From Recognition to Rise

We have listened. We have stretched. We have stepped into lives that are not our own—and returned with deeper eyes and a more open heart. "Stories that Expand Us" asked us to witness. To dismantle distance. To meet the unfamiliar not with fear but with reverence.

And now, we turn to something equally sacred—stories that help us rise. That remind us not only of our shared humanity, but of our individual power. "Stories that Empower Us" begins the return. To voice. To truth. To the parts of ourselves that were silenced, softened, or scattered—and are now ready to be reclaimed.

We move now from the act of understanding others to the practice of becoming more fully ourselves.

They Just Loved

They didn't ask
to become a debate,
a ballot box issue,
a lightning rod
for someone else's fear.

They just loved.

Quietly. Unapologetically.
In backyards and basements,
on dance floors and sidewalks,
in churches that turned them away,
and in homes they had to build from scratch.

They just loved.

They waited years to hold hands in public.
They learned early how to scan a room.
They carried grief that had no funeral.
They stayed, even when the world said *leave*.

And still—they laughed.
They married.
They made art.
They held each other
through storms both literal and human.

And all the while,
they just kept loving.

Forged in flame
Answered with voice

Part VI: Stories that Empower Us

These are the stories of rising.

Of women finding their voice,
of silence becoming sound,
of pain becoming power.

Here, we remember what we've always known —
that storytelling is
an act of reclamation.

Chapter 22: Stories that Empower Us

Not every story begins with strength. Most begin in silence, in ache, in forgetting. But somewhere along the way, something stirs.

This section comes near the end of the book not because empowerment is an afterthought—but because it is often what comes *after*: after the loss has been named, after the sorrow has been held, after the quiet return to self has begun.

Empowerment is not something handed to us. It is something we *remember*. At first quietly, then with rising certainty.

When I began writing this book, my intention was simple: to create a sanctuary of stories. A space where women could find solace, reflection, and companionship. A guide through illness, grief, transition, and confusion. And that intention still lives at the heart of every page.

But something else revealed itself along the way. This wasn't just about comfort. It was about awakening. Not just healing—but *rising*. Not just surviving—but *returning* to our inner fire.

We are living in a time of great unraveling. Systems are breaking. Old truths are shedding their disguises. And in the quiet center of it all, women are being called. To speak. To lead. To soften *and* to stand. To remember that we were never here just to be kind. We were here to be *true*.

For centuries, the feminine has been silenced, sweetened, or softened into erasure. We have been praised for nurturing but not for knowing. Loved for yielding but not for leading. But look again—at history, at the earth, at the soul of every revolution. Women have always shaped the world. What's changing is that we are no longer doing it invisibly.

This section—"Stories that Empower Us"—is not about perfection. It's about return. It's about the woman who stops apologizing for her strength. Who stops shrinking to stay safe. Who stops waiting for permission.

These stories are not about superheroes. They are about women like you. Women who trust their voice, who listen to their intuition, who hold the line or begin again. Women who rise—sometimes loudly, sometimes softly, but always truly.

And you are part of that story. Not separate from these pages—but woven into them.

This is not about trends. It is about timing. Because the world does not just need your resilience. It needs your *vision*. Your *truth*. Your *presence*.

The divine feminine is not a fad. It is the remembering of what has always been sacred: Compassion. Collaboration. Embodied knowing. The wisdom that heals instead of conquers.

So, let this section be more than stories. Let it be a threshold. Let it be a mirror. Let it be the invitation you didn't know you were waiting for.

You are not too late. You are right on time. This is the part of the story where the heroine does not disappear.

She rises.

The Women They Forgot to Tell You About

She was never powerless.
She was only forgotten.
Until now.

They told you history.
But they forgot to tell you her story.

Not the polished queens
or the saints revised for comfort.

But the women who
stitched nations back together
with calloused hands and moonlight.

The women who stopped wars,
walked miles for water,
whispered rebellion
into hungry children's ears.

The women who made
beauty out of dust.

The ones who burned,
not from shame—
but from being fire in a world
that called them fragile.
They forgot to tell you:
You come from them.

Chapter 23: Reclaiming Her Story

Empowerment Through Fiction and History

In this section, we don't simply study history; we *reclaim* it. These are not textbook names or forgotten footnotes. These are women who lived, defied, resisted, ruled, wrote, and reshaped their worlds—and now, through fiction and nonfiction alike, we remember them.

Historical fiction and creative reimaginings allow us to walk beside these women in the intimacy of story. Memoir and biography anchor those stories in lived truth. Each book in this section brings the past into our hands, helping us reclaim a lineage that has always been ours.

Some of these women stopped wars with their voices. Others lit revolutions with their refusal. Their legacies are not metaphor. They are invitation. Let these stories awaken the memory that lives in your blood.

She Stopped a War with Her Will

In 2003, as Liberia bled from civil war, Leymah Gbowee gathered women in white T-shirts and staged a silent protest outside government buildings. They called for peace, launched a sex strike, and refused to be ignored.

When negotiations stalled, Leymah locked the doors of the meeting hall. "No one leaves," she said, "until there is a deal."

There was. The war ended. Liberia elected Africa's first female president. This is the story they should have taught you.

She Dared to Say "No" to Power

In Nazi Germany, Sophie Scholl, a 21-year-old student, distributed anti-Hitler leaflets with her brother. When caught, she said, "What we wrote and said is what many people think. They just don't dare to say it."

She was executed days later. She did not flinch. And because she stood up, others began to as well.

She Made a Nation Sit Still

In 1975, 90% of Icelandic women walked off their jobs, homes, and unpaid labour for one day. They didn't cook. They didn't clean. They didn't show up. The country ground to a halt.

Five years later, Iceland elected the world's first female president.

This is what refusal can look like. This is what change can sound like.

Book Friends

Joan of Arc by Mark Twain *(historical fiction)*

A lesser-known labour of love from Twain, this novel is a meticulously researched and reverent retelling of the life of Joan of Arc, told from the perspective of a fictional childhood companion. This work honours Joan's spiritual conviction, military brilliance, and unwavering sense of destiny. It paints her not just as a martyr but as a luminous force of clarity, courage, and unshakable faith.

> *Why it helps:* This novel restores power to a historical figure often flattened into symbol or saint. It invites readers to witness Joan not just as a warrior but as a girl who trusted her inner knowing above all else—and who paid the price for being unafraid

Circe by Madeline Miller

A myth retold through the eyes of Circe, a banished nymph turned powerful witch. A luminous tale of exile, agency, and self-creation. Through isolation and magic, she reclaims her power on her own terms.

Why it helps: Because it validates the transformative journey from exile to empowerment. It encourages women to find strength in solitude and reclaim narrative control.

The Invention of Wings by Sue Monk Kidd

Inspired by real abolitionist sisters and the enslaved girl they resisted for. In a dual narrative of rebellion, sisterhood, and liberation, two women, bound by injustice, rise in their own acts of courage.

Why it helps: Because it illuminates the complexity of oppression and alliance, and empowers readers to challenge inherited systems and trust in shared acts of resistance.

Nonfiction - Courage & Conviction

While this book focuses primarily on fiction, this moment calls for something different. The women in these pages were real. Flesh and fire. Courage and conviction. Too often, their stories have been buried beneath the noise of history—or omitted altogether.

Rad Women Worldwide by KateSchatz & Miriam Klein Stahl

An illustrated celebration of 40 extraordinary women from across the globe—leaders, rebels, artists, scientists, athletes, and visionaries, many of whom remain largely unknown in traditional history books. From ancient warriors to modern activists, this book brings together a dynamic sisterhood of change-makers who defied norms and reshaped culture, often with little recognition.

Why it helps: This book offers a joyful, powerful antidote to historical erasure. Its diverse range of women—across cultures, time periods, and callings—reminds readers that greatness comes in many forms.

Mighty Be Our Powers by Leymah Gbowee

A memoir of motherhood, faith, and fierce collective action. This firsthand account of Liberia's women's peace movement shows how spiritual courage and community organizing ended a war—and launched a nation's rebirth.

> *Why it helps:* Because it demonstrates the unstoppable power of grassroots women's leadership, and encourages readers to believe in peace-building and purpose from within.

Sophie Scholl and the White Rose by Annette Dumbach & Jud Newborn

A powerful account of Sophie Scholl's nonviolent resistance to Nazi tyranny. Her refusal to stay silent became a lightning rod for youth-led activism in Germany.

> *Why it helps:* Because it shows that even brief, defiant action can echo for generations, and encourages moral clarity and brave speech in the face of fear.

She Has Always Been the Fire

You were never just
the reader of stories.
You were born from
story-shapers.

From mothers who taught resistance in lullabies,
grandmothers who brewed wisdom into bone broth,
aunties who read poems instead of prayers,
daughters who rose before the world was ready.

Let no one tell you again
that your power must be earned.
It was already paid for—
in sweat,

in silence,
in sacrifice.

And now, at last,
it is remembered.

Chapter 24: Voice as Visibility

The Truth Beneath Silence

Some silences are sacred. But many are not.

Many are survival. Many are suppression. Many were learned—through shaming, interruption, dismissal, punishment. Through mothers who never said how they felt. Through fathers who didn't ask. Through cultures that told women: Be agreeable. Be quiet. Be grateful.

This silence is not emptiness; it is full. Full of things unspoken. Full of the truths we weren't ready—or allowed—to say. And yet, beneath that silence lives a voice. Soft at first, then steady, then sovereign.

This section is for the woman who was taught to speak only when spoken to. Who edited herself to keep the peace. Who stayed silent to keep a job. Or a marriage. Or a mask. It is for the woman who knew the truth—about harm, about brilliance, about her own worth—long before she had the language to name it.

These stories speak to her. They model what it means to break the contract of complicity. They show us how to use our voice not for noise, but for impact. To speak not just *against* what's wrong but *on behalf of* what matters. Because silence may have protected us once. But truth is what will set us free.

Book Friends

The Group by Mary McCarthy
Following eight Vassar graduates in the 1930s, this novel dissects the emotional, sexual, and intellectual constraints placed on educated women—and the quiet revolt simmering beneath.

Why it helps: Because it captures the cultural silencing of ambition and emotion and shows how women begin to claim power, even when society says no.

The Lost Apothecary by Sarah Penner

In eighteenth-century London, a secret apothecary shop dispenses poisons to women seeking justice against the men who have wronged them. Two centuries later, a modern-day historian uncovers the clues—and the voices—of those who refused to be erased.

Why it helps: Because it honours the subversive power of women's stories—especially the ones hidden, whispered, or buried in time. A tale of resistance, remembrance, and the courage to write your truth into history.

The Women Could Fly by Megan Giddings

In a dystopian world where women can be tried as witches for being nonconforming or unmarried past thirty, Josephine navigates the societal expectations that threaten to silence her and embarks on a magical, defiant journey of self-definition.

Why it helps: Because it reveals how patriarchy weaponizes both silence and suspicion, and how reclaiming voice—especially as a woman of colour—is a radical act of freedom, identity, and magic.

The Paris Library by Janet Skeslien Charles

Inspired by the true story of the American Library in Paris during WWII, this novel follows women who use books to resist both occupation and silence.

Why it helps: Because it celebrates the subtle forms of defiance—literary, emotional, and relational—that allow women to reclaim their truth even in oppressive times.

A Woman Is No Man by Etaf Rum

A multigenerational story of Palestinian American women navigating honour, silence, and inherited trauma in a conservative family structure.

Why it helps: Because it powerfully portrays how cultural and familial expectations suppress female voice—and how speaking up can break generations of silence.

The Sentence by Louise Erdrich

Set in a Minneapolis bookstore haunted by the ghost of a former customer, this novel follows Tookie, an Indigenous woman grappling with life after incarceration, the ghosts of the past, and the silence of grief and guilt.

Why it helps: Because it explores voice after trauma: how a woman reclaims her presence and truth after being silenced by both the system and her own story.

How Women Learn to Disappear

Not all vanishing acts are physical.

Women learn to disappear long before they go quiet.

We learn to take up less space. To second-guess our knowing. To defer, delay, or decorate the truth so it doesn't offend.

We learn it in classrooms where the boys interrupt. In boardrooms where our ideas are echoed back in lower registers. In families where anger is dangerous and boundaries are betrayal. In marriages where silence is mistaken for love.

We become expert shapeshifters—reading tone, room, mood, and threat with surgical precision. We apologize for things we didn't do. We edit brilliance to make it less threatening. We protect others from the truth we carry.

But invisibility comes at a cost. You cannot keep shrinking and expect to feel whole.

This book, and this chapter, is a quiet rebellion. A reminder that your voice is not too loud. Your knowing is not too much. And your story was never meant to stay silent.

She Didn't Say It Then

She didn't say it then.
Not when the moment cracked open.
Not when the lie sat unchallenged.
Not when her body burned with knowing.

She bit her tongue.
Pressed her palms.
Watched herself fold into silence
like it was a favor.

She told herself:
Now isn't the time.
They wouldn't understand.
It will make things worse.

And so the moment passed—
but the truth stayed.
Lodged beneath the ribs.
A single ember,
glowing through the years.

Until one day,
without warning or permission,
her voice returned.

And it didn't ask
for kindness
or consensus.

It simply said:
I'm still here.
And I remember.

Chapter 25: Leadership, Remembered

We've been taught that leadership looks a certain way—loud, visible, commanding. But for many women, leadership has never looked like that. It has looked like holding things together. Like guiding without recognition. Like staying soft in systems built to harden.

When a woman leads from within, it often doesn't look like leadership at all—at least not by traditional standards. It isn't about control. It isn't about visibility. It's about *truth*.

This is the kind of leadership that happens in kitchens and clinics, on school runs and night shifts, in caregiving and in boardrooms. It's the mother who raises a generation with compassion. The teacher who believes in a child no one else sees. The nurse who steadies a patient's hand. The woman who walks away from what no longer aligns—and calls that her act of power.

Leadership is not always strategic. Sometimes, it is deeply spiritual. It is the moment we choose presence over performance, alignment over approval, truth over silence.

This is what leadership becomes when a woman remembers who she is—and leads from that place. It may not fit the mold, but it reshapes the world.

What Feminine Leadership Looks Like

Holding space: creating emotional safety without fixing or performing

Naming the unsaid: articulating what others only sense

Sensing timing: knowing when to speak and when to wait

Setting boundaries: saying no without guilt, because your yes is sacred

Walking away: leading not by staying, but by choosing soul over sacrifice

Staying soft: choosing openness even when the world demands armour

Trusting the inner yes even when no one else understands it yet: This isn't passive. It isn't soft in the way we've been told soft is weak. It is rooted. It is quiet power. It is the kind of leadership that shifts things from the inside out.

The Crown Within

We've been told that leadership is earned. But what if it's remembered? What if it lives in the way we say no with clarity, hold the line with kindness, or choose stillness over spectacle?

This is the quiet crown. It's not given. It's not granted. It's claimed—by listening to the voice within, and daring to follow it home.

Book Friends

These novels portray leadership not as dominance or performance, but as alignment, presence, and self-trust. These characters don't always seek to lead. They simply refuse to betray their knowing—and, in doing so, the change the world around them.

The Priory of the Orange Tree by Samantha Shannon

In a world on the brink of chaos, Ead—a hidden priestess with quiet power—guards the queen from the shadows, guided not by ambition but by sacred duty and deep intuition. Her strength isn't loud—it's rooted, reverent, and unshakable.

> ***Why it helps:*** Because it shows how feminine strength can be grounded in spiritual clarity and

steady devotion—not conquest or control. Ead leads not by force, but by knowing when and how to act in alignment.

Wild and Distant Seas by Tara Karr Roberts

This lyrical, multigenerational novel traces the lineage of women connected by intuition, silence, and survival. From Newfoundland to coastal Maine, each woman must navigate love, loss, and legacy by trusting the pull of her own knowing.

> *Why it helps:* Because it honours the generational thread of feminine intuition—and shows how quiet, internal leadership can ripple through time, shaping lives even in the absence of recognition.

The Curse of Chalion by Lois McMaster Bujold

Set in a richly imagined world of political intrigue and divine intervention, this novel follows a protagonist who serves a powerful woman whose leadership is shaped by discernment, not dominance. She leads through her deep moral compass and unwavering sense of what is right.

> *Why it helps:* Because it reminds us that intuition is a form of intelligence—and true leadership often means choosing the less obvious, but more soul-aligned, path.

The Power by Naomi Alderman

Women across the globe suddenly develop the ability to emit electrical energy from their bodies, tipping the balance of global power. But as strength shifts, questions of ethics, intuition, and restraint rise.

> *Why it helps:* Because it explores what happens when power is divorced from integrity—and reminds us that true leadership must be anchored in internal wisdom, not external force.

State of Wonder by Ann Patchett

Pharmacologist Marina Singh travels deep into the Amazon to investigate a colleague's death and confront her elusive mentor, Dr. Annick Swenson. What unfolds is a gripping journey through scientific ambition, ethical dilemmas, and the complexities of female leadership.

> *Why it helps:* This novel explores what it means for a woman to lead—alone, unapologetically, and on her own terms. It reveals the tension between care and control, ambition and responsibility, and invites readers to reflect on the high cost—and quiet courage—of holding power.

Matrix by Lauren Groff

Inspired by the life of twelfth-century poet and mystic Marie de France, this novel follows a young woman cast out of court and into the abbey, where she transforms a struggling convent into a place of feminine power. Her leadership blends mysticism, intuition, and fierce devotion to her chosen community.

> *Why it helps:* Because it reimagines leadership as mystical stewardship. Marie doesn't seize power—she midwifes it, shaping a new world by listening inwardly and leading from sacred vision.

She Knew When to Rise

She didn't rise for the applause.
Or the title.
Or the chance to prove herself again.

She rose because her knowing said:
Now.

She rose after the silence.
After the sitting still.
After the world told her
to wait her turn and lower her gaze.

She rose from intuition–
not ambition.
From truth–
not urgency.

And when she stood,
she didn't tower.
She didn't shout.

She simply became
undeniable.

And the room,
the rhythm,
the very ground beneath her–shifted.
Not because she took power.
But because she remembered
she had it.

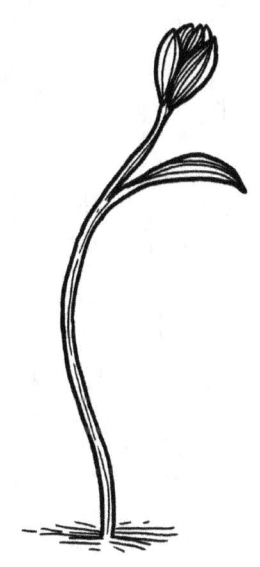

*You are not arriving—you are remembering
The return was always within you*

Part VII: The Sacred Return

This is the place we've been heading toward —
not back to the beginning,
but forward into wholeness.

Gratitude.
Joy.
The voice that returns.

This is the sacred return —
not a destination,
but a frequency.

And it lives in you.

Chapter 26: The Sacred Return

There comes a moment in every woman's life—not once, but many times—when something deep begins to stir. It may not announce itself clearly. It may arrive as restlessness, as grief, as a quiet ache. But it comes. A whisper beneath the noise that says: *This isn't the whole of me.*

This final section is for that moment. For that gentle rising. For the remembering.

Throughout this book, we've explored fiction as sanctuary, medicine, and mirror. We've moved through stories that comfort, awaken, reflect, and expand. But now, we are not just turning another page. We are returning—not to who we were, but to who we've always been beneath the roles, the rushing, the forgetting.

This is not a single insight. It is a homecoming.

The Sacred Return is a threshold. A place of soft clarity. It honors the wisdom we carry as women—not in spite of our wounds, but because of the way we have risen through them. Here, fiction becomes something more than story. It becomes ceremony. Compass. Permission.

We begin with **intuition**—that ancient knowing that lives in the body, the breath, the silence before the thought. So many women have been taught to doubt it. But in truth, it is the most natural compass we possess. Fiction strengthens this inner voice by offering stories that echo what we already sense: *I knew that, before I knew how I knew it.*

Next comes **surrender**—so often mistaken for passivity, when in fact it is a profound form of wisdom. In the lives of the women we read about, surrender marks the moment they stop running from themselves. When they release the need to earn what was always theirs. It is not weakness. It is trust.

Compassion, too, is redefined here. Not the self-erasing kind. Not the performance. But the fierce kind—the kind that sets boundaries, speaks truth, and holds presence without abandoning self. This is the compassion that says: *I will not disappear to keep the peace.*

Gratitude, in its sacred form, is also part of the return. Not forced optimism, but reverent seeing. The kind born of survival and clarity. It says: *Even in all I've lost, I know what remains.* Fiction reminds us of this kind of gratitude. It helps us hold ache and awe in the same breath.

And always, there is **voice**. Not always loud, but always true. Too often, women have been praised for being agreeable. For being quiet. But voice is not just volume. It is presence. It is essence. This return is where the voice comes back—not only for ourselves, but for the women who could not speak, the daughters who are watching, the inner girl who is still listening.

We arrive, too, at **age**—not as decline, but as revelation. Aging is not the closing of the story; it is where many of the most powerful chapters begin. Here, we live not for approval, but from essence. Not by roles, but by rhythm. Fiction reminds us that the second act is where transformation often takes root.

J.R.R. Tolkien gave us a word for a moment we often struggle to name: **eucatastrophe**. It means the sudden turn toward good. The moment when, after all seems lost, something unexpected arrives—not to erase the sorrow, but to shift the weight of it. It is not a tidy ending. It is the grace we didn't see coming.

The Sacred Return holds space for this turn. Not as guarantee, but as possibility. As soul-truth: even in the darkest stories, light can find a way through. Fiction teaches this better than almost anything else. It lets us feel despair fully—and still believe in the arrival of something redemptive.

These stories don't promise rescue. But they do promise revelation. They say: *stay.* Stay long enough to witness what might yet become beautiful. Stay until the moment arrives—not when everything is fixed, but when something holy breaks through. Because healing, too, has its eucatastrophes.

CHAPTER 26: THE SACRED RETURN

And then, there is **joy**. Joy is often misunderstood. Mistaken for a fleeting high, or a reward for endurance. But real joy—deep, rooted joy—is not about avoiding pain. It is about remembering aliveness. It's the soul's quiet yes. The breath that returns after heartbreak. The light that comes not because all is perfect, but because something sacred within you has survived.

This joy is not naïve. It knows sorrow. It has sat beside grief and still dares to laugh. It has faced endings and still chooses wonder. In a world that worships productivity, joy is a revolution. It says: *I am worthy of delight. Even now. Especially now.*

The stories in this section help us reclaim joy not as decoration, but as devotion. They remind us that we do not have to earn it. That we are allowed to feel good, even in a fractured world. That joy is not selfish—it is sustaining. And that pleasure, play, beauty, and laughter are not distractions from healing. They are healing.

The Sacred Return is the weaving of these truths—intuition, surrender, compassion, gratitude, voice, age, eucatastrophe, and joy—into one grounded offering. Not as trend, but as timeless feminine wisdom. Not as spiritual escape, but as soulful embodiment. Not as conclusion, but as invitation.

As Clarissa Pinkola Estés wrote in *Women Who Run with the Wolves*, this return is a deep remembering. A rhythm. A reclamation of the wild and the wise. A homecoming to our original knowing—the kind that never needed permission to exist.

The stories in this section are not only beautiful; they are restorative. They invite us to trust our becoming. They remind us that softness is strength, that clarity is power, and that our presence—fully owned—is sacred.

This is not the end of the book. It is the beginning of your own deeper chapter.

She Is the Divine Feminine

She is not a whisper—
she is the first sound.

The breath behind the wind,
the silence between stars.

She is water—shaping stone without force.
She is earth—everything grows through her.

Not soft from weakness,
but because she chooses not to harden.

She knows—
before the words,
before the proof.

Her power opens.
Her love remembers.
Her truth resonates.

She rises now—
not to conquer,
but to restore.
Not a goddess to worship—
a mirror to remember.

You are her.
She is you.

Chapter 27:
The Compass Within

There is a knowing that doesn't explain itself. It arrives before the logic. Before the facts line up. Before the plan makes sense. Intuition is not impulse or fear. It is the body's language for truth—a language most women were taught to forget.

We were trained to override the pause, to second-guess the no, and to silence the soft tug toward something that made no sense... except to the part of us that already knew.

Trauma can sever us from this compass. When something overwhelms or violates our sense of safety, we stop listening—not because the intuition is gone, but because survival required us to turn the volume down. And yet... the body remembers. And intuition waits.

It doesn't shout. It doesn't plead. It doesn't arrive with credentials or clarity. It whispers, gently but firmly: *This way. Not that.* When we learn to listen again, we return to a deeper kind of safety. One that isn't imposed, but remembered.

This section is a reclaiming. A quiet restoration of trust in the oldest compass you've ever had.

A Story of Spidey Sense and Survival

For nearly two decades, I traveled the world through my work—often solo, often extending trips to explore far-flung places on my own. Looking back, I know what kept me safe wasn't fear. It was intuition. That quiet tug. That pause. The whisper that said: *Not this. Not now.*

As a young woman traveling alone, I sometimes felt that subtle inner shift when something was off. One night in Greece, a man followed me through winding streets after I refused his persistent invitations. I ducked into a small shop where two women stood behind the counter. I told them what was happening.

They made me coffee. Brought out a stool. Pretended I was an old friend. Kept me safe. They never questioned my story. They trusted my knowing—because they had one, too. I've never forgotten their kindness. And I've never stopped listening.

Intuition doesn't ask you to explain. It asks you to trust what you feel—before the world gives you permission to believe it.

Book Friends
Women's Intuition by Lisa Samson
After years of conforming to the roles expected of her, Larkspur finds herself untethered—by circumstance and by choice. As she steps away from the life she was told to want, she begins to hear the stirrings of her own intuition—faint at first, then clearer, like music beneath the noise.

> *Why it helps:* Because it gently affirms what many women know but rarely name—that the most sacred awakenings often begin with quiet discontent. This story honours the slow, unglamorous process of returning to the self—not through crisis, but through soulful, ordinary courage.

The Passion of Artemisia by Susan Vreeland
Based on the true story of Artemisia Gentileschi, a 17th-century painter who overcame betrayal, trauma, and societal silencing to become one of the most revered artists of her time.

> *Why it helps:* Because it celebrates the courage it takes for a woman to trust her truth, especially in a world that punishes her for speaking it. Artemisia's story reminds us that creative and intuitive power are acts of resistance in themselves.

***The Island of Missing Trees* by Elif Shafak**
Told through the intertwined voices of a teenage girl and a fig tree, this novel explores the inherited intuition of a daughter navigating grief, identity, and ancestral silence.

> ***Why it helps:*** Because it reminds us that intuition is not only personal; it's also intergenerational. Even what was never spoken aloud lives in the body and can guide us toward healing.

The Art of Intuition* by Sophy Burnham *(non-fiction)
A luminous exploration of how intuition speaks—through images, hunches, dreams, synchronicities, and the quiet nudges we often dismiss. Blending memoir, mysticism, and research, Burnham invites us to reclaim what she calls the "lost sense," and to see intuition not as a vague feeling, but as a sacred form of inner knowing. Her writing is spacious, accessible, and filled with stories that echo with ancient wisdom.

> ***Why it helps:*** Because it validates the quiet signals we often overlook. This book is a gentle, affirming guide for those learning to trust the soft voice within—the compass that points not just to answers, but to alignment.

Intuition as Energetic Knowing

So often, we speak of intuition as if it were fleeting—a whisper, a hunch, a mysterious instinct we can't quite explain. But what if it's more than that? What if intuition is not just a mystical flicker but a *form of energetic intelligence*—shaped by both biology and by our connection to something greater?

Both Dr. Joe Dispenza and Lynne McTaggart explore this possibility, weaving together neuroscience, quantum physics, and consciousness research to suggest that intuitive insight is not abstract mysticism. It is measurable. Trainable. And deeply personal.

In *The Field*, McTaggart presents a compelling body of research suggesting we are part of a quantum information network—a subtle matrix in which thoughts, emotions, and even intentions influence matter. Intuition, in this view, is not guesswork. It is resonance, a form of deep listening that occurs beyond language, rooted in the body and attuned to the invisible threads that connect us all.

Dr. Joe Dispenza brings this understanding closer to the physical self. His work shows that when we quiet the analytical mind and enter heart-brain coherence, we access a deeper state of awareness—one where decision-making becomes less reactive and more aligned. In this space, intuition is not irrational. It is embodied knowing. Clear. Trustworthy. Accurate.

Together, these teachings remind us that gut feelings are not emotional static. They are *wisdom signals*. The body, after all, is often the first to sense what the mind has not yet named.

Chapter 28: The Grace of Surrender

Surrender is not giving up. It is laying down what we were never meant to carry alone. It's the loosening of our grip—on control, identity, urgency, and outcomes—and the quiet return to presence. To breath. To enoughness.

This section is for the woman who has tried everything. Who has held too much, for too long. For the caregiver whose body whispers *rest*. For the achiever who no longer wants to prove. For the seeker learning to trust life again—even when the timing feels all wrong.

Surrender is not passivity. It is participation without resistance. It is releasing the illusion of control in favor of the deeper rhythm that has always moved beneath the surface.

More than once, surrender has saved me. Not in the cinematic way, but quietly. Through exhaustion. Through delay. Through disappointment. Through the spiritual wrestling that arises when life doesn't move as fast as your vision. When applications go out and doors stay closed. When the *yes* hasn't arrived. When the work is ready but the world isn't.

That's when I remember: divine timing is its own form of grace. The pause is not punishment. It is alignment in disguise.

More than thirty years ago, a wise friend introduced me to a phrase that has never left me:

Focused surrender. Commit fully—and then let go.

This paradox, introduced in *The Life We Are Given* and echoed in *Mastery* by George Leonard, became a quiet compass. It taught me that surrender isn't the end of effort—it is what gives effort meaning.

Surrender is feminine wisdom. An ancient, intuitive knowing that says: *I trust what is unfolding. I do not need to push the river.*

This section is a soft exhale. A space to unclench, to stop striving—not because you've failed, but because you've already arrived.

Let surrender be a quiet power. Let it walk beside you like a friend. Let it remind you: There is strength in not forcing, and there is peace in trusting that what is meant will come—when the soil is ready, and the soul is too.

Book Friends
The Lightkeeper's Daughters by Jean E. Pendziwol
A lyrical, slowly unfolding story of memory, forgiveness, and uncovering truth in later years. Set against the haunting beauty of Lake Superior, it weaves past and present through the voices of two women: one young, one nearing the end of her life.

> *Why it helps:* It reminds us that it's never too late to release the past and reclaim peace—a gentle invitation to let go of what no longer needs to be held, and to find resolution in the stories we once buried.

The Namesake by Jhumpa Lahiri
A beautifully crafted novel about identity, belonging, and the quiet surrender required to live between cultures and expectations. Through the life of Gogol Ganguli, Lahiri explores the ache of never quite fitting and the grace that comes with embracing ambiguity.

> *Why it helps:* It shows how surrender isn't weakness, but wisdom—especially when navigating identity, family, and the spaces in between. For anyone learning to honour both inheritance and individuality, this story speaks softly but profoundly.

The Garden of Evening Mists by Tan Twan Eng
Set in postwar Malaya, this haunting and elegant novel explores trauma, surrender to beauty, and healing through presence

and landscape. At its heart is a garden—a space of silence, symmetry, and slow recovery.

> ***Why it helps:*** It offers a meditative reflection on how beauty and stillness can become vessels for grief, acceptance, and renewal. For those carrying sorrow in the body, this story is a quiet balm.

Still Life by Sarah Winman

An epic and unexpectedly joyful story of art, war, and the long arc of fate. Its characters cross borders, decades, and heartbreak, surrendering not to despair but to the deep, surprising goodness of life.

> ***Why it helps:*** It celebrates the serendipity and slow unfolding of life, reminding us that some of the best things arrive unforced and unplanned. A generous novel that affirms joy as a kind of trust.

The Bookshop by Penelope Fitzgerald

A poignant, quietly powerful tale of one woman's resilience in a resistant town—where surrender comes not in defeat, but in the dignity of grace. Fitzgerald's sparse prose leaves space for the emotional weight of every choice.

> ***Why it helps:*** It reflects the emotional truth that sometimes surrender is simply honoring our limits—and still standing with quiet integrity. For those who've tried, persisted, and chosen peace, this novel offers a kind mirror.

When She Let Go

She loosened her grip—
not because she gave up,
but because she remembered
she didn't have to hold it all.

She unknotted her expectations,
unfastened her urgency,
let the timelines unravel
like thread from an old spool.

She didn't fall.
She floated—
on the current of something
wiser than will.

And when the voice of not-yet
echoed louder than now,
she whispered back:
"I trust you, Life."

Not in the way
one trusts perfection—
but in the way
a tree trusts autumn,
even as it lets its leaves go.

The Paradox of Surrender

Surrender is one of the most misunderstood spiritual principles, and is often confused with weakness, passivity, or resignation. But true surrender is not about doing nothing. It's about aligning our energy with what *is*, instead of endlessly fighting what *isn't*.

George Leonard, in *The Life We Are Given*, offers a powerful reframe: "Commit fully. Then let go." This is the paradox: effort and release, intention and allowance, devotion and detachment.

Feminine wisdom traditions have long known this: that surrender is not a collapse but a cooperation with the invisible forces moving through our lives. It is where grace meets groundedness.

When we surrender, we don't stop dreaming. We simply stop demanding. And in that space, life often delivers what striving never could.

Chapter 29: Fierce Compassion

We're taught that compassion is gentle. That to be kind is to stay quiet, flexible, agreeable. But real compassion—fierce compassion—is something else entirely.

It doesn't just comfort. It protects. It draws the line when others cross it. It says, *"This far, and no further."*

Fierce compassion doesn't abandon softness. It anchors it. It allows us to stay present without losing ourselves—to say no without guilt, and to choose love without allowing harm.

For many women, this kind of compassion arrives later in life—when the desire to please finally loosens its grip and the need to live truthfully takes root. We begin to learn: That we can love people deeply and still hold boundaries. That we can be nurturing without disappearing. That compassion is not martyrdom. It is clarity.

This chapter honours the women who have stood in that clarity. Who have left relationships that drained them. Who have said yes to caregiving while refusing to be erased by it. Who have fought not just for themselves, but for others—for truth, for justice, for dignity, and for the right to rest.

Fierce compassion is not loud. It does not need applause. But it does ask something of us: That we tell the truth. That we love ourselves in equal measure. And that we never mistake silence for grace. Because real compassion doesn't always feel good. But it always leads toward wholeness.

Book Friends
The Way: A Girl Who Dared to Rise **by Kristen Wolf**
In ancient Palestine, a young woman escapes oppression and finds power in a secret sisterhood that teaches her to question everything.

> *Why it helps:* A bold reimagining of spiritual truth and inner strength, reminding us that compassion and courage often rise together.

Dream Count by Chimamanda Ngozi Adichie

The lives of four African women unfold against a backdrop of betrayal, kinship, and cultural upheaval, each navigating compassion in deeply personal ways.

> *Why it helps:* It illuminates how tenderness and truth endure—even in places that try to silence both.

My Name Is Emilia del Valle by Isabel Allende

A journalist and reformer in 19th-century San Francisco defies patriarchal systems in her fight for justice and dignity.

> *Why it helps:* A powerful example of how compassion becomes activism—and how voice becomes change.

Bel Canto by Ann Patchett

At a lavish embassy party turned hostage crisis, unlikely bonds form between captors and captives. Music becomes a quiet thread of connection as tension gives way to tenderness.

> *Why it helps:* A haunting meditation on how empathy and beauty can surface even in the most perilous of places. It reminds us that compassion is possible, even where fear and power collide.

Love, with Edges

Love, she learned,
didn't mean bleeding quietly.
It didn't mean bending so far
she forgot the shape of her spine.

Love, real love,
could be warm—and still have walls.
It could open its arms
and still close its doors.

She began to understand
that compassion with no edges
was not kindness—
it was erasure.

So she drew a line,
not in anger,
but in reverence
for the space she had reclaimed.

And when they said
she had changed,
she smiled.

Because she had.
She had become
a woman who loved
without leaving herself behind.

The Healing Power of Compassion

Compassion is more than a virtue. It is a biological balm—one of the most powerful medicines we carry.

When we extend care to another, especially in times of distress or vulnerability, the body doesn't simply witness the act—it responds. Oxytocin rises, stress hormones recede, and heart rate variability increases, signaling a shift toward physiological calm. We become less inflamed, less anxious, less alone in our own nervous system. In this way, compassion is not just for the receiver. It nourishes the giver too.

But here's what many of us were never taught: Compassion that is constant and unbound can become depleting. When we pour endlessly from our cup—without replenishment, without boundary, without breath—what once healed becomes what hollows.

So the question becomes: How do we care deeply without collapsing? How do we offer presence without forgetting our own?

The answer lies not in less compassion—but in wiser compassion. The kind that knows when to lean in, and when to step back. The kind that understands: You are not meant to carry everyone. You are meant to stand beside them, rooted in your own steadiness.

Compassion is not just something you give. It's something you *practice*. With intention. With boundaries. With rituals that return you to yourself.

Because when compassion is offered with wisdom, it becomes sustainable. It becomes sacred. And it becomes, quite literally, medicine for the soul.

Chapter 30: The Voice that Returns

There comes a moment in every woman's life when silence grows too heavy to bear. When staying agreeable begins to feel like self-abandonment. When the cost of invisibility is no longer worth the quiet it preserves.

This is the moment of return.

For the woman who was taught to stay small. Who became fluent in deflection, in politeness, in disappearing. Who learned to rewrite her truth in order to be more palatable. Who became so practiced in swallowing her voice, she forgot what it sounded like.

And yet—beneath all the years of quiet—something endured. A flicker. A pulse. A heat in the chest that whispered: *This isn't the whole of me.*

To speak, to be seen, and to name your truth—especially as a woman—has always been radical. Because when women speak honestly, the room changes. The family shifts. The culture trembles. And not everyone wants that. This is why your voice may have been called too loud, too emotional, too dramatic, too sensitive, too much.

But your voice was never the problem. The world simply wasn't ready for its honesty.

This is not a chapter of confrontation. This is a chapter of *reclamation*. Because becoming visible is not vanity. It is presence. It is a return to selfhood. It is claiming space in a world that has too often asked you to shrink.

And truth? Truth is not just fact. It is a compass. It is the steady rhythm beneath your ribs. It is the sound of your soul remembering its shape.

Let this be the moment you stop apologizing. Let this be the chapter where your story steps fully into the light. Because you are not too much. You are finally becoming whole.

Book Friends
Tilda Is Visible by Jane Tara
A magical realist gem about a woman who becomes literally visible only after stepping into her truth. Tilda's journey of self-visibility and personal awakening speaks to every woman who's ever felt unseen, overlooked, or erased.

> *Why it helps:* A playful yet poignant reminder that reclaiming voice is often the first step toward reclaiming presence—and the courage to be fully seen. It invites us to consider how invisibility is often a byproduct of emotional erasure, not personal failure.

10 Minutes 38 Seconds in This Strange World by Elif Shafak
This lyrical, haunting novel follows a woman's thoughts in the ten minutes after death. In that liminal space, she reclaims her truth and dares to be remembered. A searing story about silencing, survival, and the persistence of voice.

> *Why it helps:* It affirms that even after life's deepest betrayals, the soul seeks—and often finds—a way to be heard. A tribute to voice as legacy, this novel underscores how bearing witness to one life can illuminate the silence around many.

The Paper Palace by Miranda Cowley Heller
A woman faces a life-altering decision while reckoning with the secrets she's carried for decades. A portrait of a woman unearthing her voice, layer by buried layer. Its setting, both idyllic and charged, becomes the emotional landscape for revelation.

> *Why it helps:* A deeply human exploration of how voice is shaped by choice, silence, and memory—and what it takes to speak your truth at last. It reminds readers that even long-held silence can be broken with integrity, honesty, and heart.

How Beautiful We Were by Imbolo Mbue

Set in a fictional African village exploited by an American oil company, this novel follows the unfolding resistance of its people—particularly a courageous young girl whose quiet defiance becomes the voice of a movement.

> *How it helps:* Because it shows how the quiet, steady voice of truth—once awakened—can dismantle silence, restore agency, and shape an entirely different future.

When Women Were Dragons by Kelly Barnhill

In an alternate 1950s America, a mass phenomenon known as the "Dragoning" causes thousands of women to spontaneously transform into dragons—shedding the silence, shame, and societal expectations that once bound them. Through one girl's coming-of-age in the aftermath, this genre-defying novel explores memory, rage, and the quiet inheritance of resistance.

> *Why it helps:* A bold, imaginative allegory of feminine power reclaimed. For any woman who's been told to contain her voice, this story offers fierce permission to expand, speak, and soar. It's not just about transformation—it's about remembering the fire that was always there.

She Spoke Anyway

They told her she was too much.
Too bold. Too bright. Too bruised.

So she learned to whisper
when she wanted to roar.
To nod
when she longed to disagree.
To smile
when her soul ached for silence.

She made herself smaller
so others could feel big.
Made herself softer
so the world could stay hard.

But something inside her
refused to disappear.

A pulse. A page.
A fire that flickered, waiting.
And one day, without warning,
she stopped apologizing
for her tone, her tears, her truth.

She spoke anyway.
Not for revenge.
Not for applause.
But because silence had become a cage
and her voice—the only key.

The Risk of Voice

There's a reason you were taught to be quiet. To soften your opinion. To reframe your feelings. To make things easier for everyone else. It wasn't because your voice was wrong. It was because your truth made the room uncomfortable. But comfort is not the same as safety. And silence is not the same as peace.

Speaking your truth may shift relationships. It may stretch your world. But it will also set you free.

You don't owe anyone your invisibility. You owe yourself the sound of your own voice.

Chapter 31: Aging as Awakening

The Wisdom Keepers

In many Indigenous traditions, elders are not forgotten—they are followed. They are the keepers of land memory, of spiritual rhythm, of truths not written in books but carried in breath. When they speak, it is not to dwell on the past—it is to ground the present in something deeper.

In Japan, the aesthetic of *wabi-sabi* sees beauty not in flawlessness but in the gentle dignity of imperfection. A crack in a teacup isn't damage—it's history. Proof that something has endured, has held, has mattered.

In Hindu tradition, the later years of life are called *vanaprastha*—a sacred stage not of retreat but of reflection. A time to guide, and to walk the inner forest with reverence, not retreat.

In Māori culture, the *kaumātua*—the elders—are honoured not because they hold power but because they *hold presence*. Their wisdom isn't archived; it's lived.

In Ghana, when an elder woman enters the room, others rise—not out of politeness, but out of awe. Her silver hair is not a sign of fading. It is the crown of one who holds the weight of memory, time, and moral clarity. She is not past her prime—she is *in* it. Around the world, reverence for age is instinctive. But here, in much of the Western world, it is nearly extinct.

I was sixty-seven when people began to ask when I would retire—as if my value came with an expiration date. But I didn't feel finished. I felt *ready*. Ready for deeper work, fuller expression, unapologetic truth. Still, the culture began to look through me.

I have a friend, seventy-five, who has lived in over eighty countries, taught in universities, written books, and is currently about to publish another. She is vibrant, sharp, and still reaching. And yet, she struggles to find kindred spirits, because so many her age have been taught to shrink, to settle, to stop. She doesn't want to garden her days away. She wants to bloom *within* them.

Another friend, seventy, once the strong center of her family and career, now finds herself adrift. With grown children and a life of service behind her, she wonders what comes next. Culture tells her she's fading. But I know she's just ripening.

Because I have seen the truth, and I have *lived* it: This is not the end. This is the return. The return to essence. To soul. To the self that no longer needs to prove, but only to *be*. Not invisible. But invincible. And, finally, free.

Book Friends

The stories that follow offer fictional mirrors for this sacred season of life. They centre on women who are not fading but evolving—who are still dreaming, still daring, still becoming. These characters remind us that it's never too late to begin again.

Lillian Boxfish Takes a Walk by Kathleen Rooney

Eighty-five-year-old Lillian wanders Manhattan on New Year's Eve, revisiting her rich past as a poet and advertising legend. Witty, sharp, and full of life.

> *Why it helps:* Because it shows that memory, wit, and a walking stick can be tools of liberation—and that reflection is its own kind of power.

An Elderly Lady Is Up to No Good by Helene Tursten

Sharp, solitary, and subversive stories of an older woman who does not go quietly. With wit as dry as her conscience is clear, she navigates life—and the occasional crime—on her own unapologetic terms.

Why it helps: Because it shatters stereotypes of the elderly as docile or passive, offering a delightfully dark form of autonomy and defiance. It reminds us that age is not the end of agency—but a bold, unapologetic continuation of it.

The Little Old Lady Who Broke All the Rules by Catharina Ingelman-Sundberg

A group of seniors rebel against invisibility with wit and mischief. What begins as a quiet discontent turns into a charmingly orchestrated crime spree for justice and joy.

Why it helps: Because it reframes aging as irreverent, communal, and creatively rebellious—a playful revolt against invisibility.

How to Age Disgracefully by Clare Pooley

When 80-year-old Edith decides she's not done living—truly living—she swaps quiet resignation for bold rebellion. Alongside a mismatched group of companions, she finds herself dismantling ageist expectations, making unexpected connections, and rediscovering her voice in the most unlikely ways.

Why it helps: Because aging isn't a retreat—it's a return. To vitality. To voice. To the self that existed before the world told you to shrink. This heartwarming, funny, and spirited novel reminds us that awakening isn't reserved for the young—it's available at every age, especially when we dare to age on our own terms.

Radiant Rebellion* by Karen Walrond *(nonfiction)
Part manifesto, part memoir, this luminous book reframes aging as a radical act of self-definition. With warmth and bold clarity, Walrond explores joy, purpose, and unapologetic presence in the second half of life. She invites women to stand tall in their stories—not in spite of their age, but *because* of it.

> ***Why it helps:*** Because it invites women to reclaim aging as an act of sovereignty and radiance—to live not smaller, but brighter, and to honour their visibility, vitality, and voice as sacred.

Breaking the Age Code* by Becca Levy *(nonfiction)
This groundbreaking work weaves scientific research with human stories to show how our beliefs about aging shape how we age. Levy, a leading Yale researcher, reveals that the way we think about growing older can directly impact our health, memory, and even lifespan—and that reframing those beliefs can be a powerful tool for transformation.

> ***Why it helps:*** Because it affirms, with science, what wisdom traditions have always known: that aging is not decay—it's dynamic. And that a single shift in perspective can become a form of healing.

She is Not Done

There is a myth that aging is a slow disappearance. But what if it's the opposite? What if, with every year, we become more visible to ourselves?

Not the self who sought approval. Not the one who kept quiet to keep peace. But the self who remembers—what she loves, what she believes, what she knows in her bones.

Aging is not retreat. It is revelation. It is the shedding of what no longer fits. It is the return of voice, of vision, of value not measured by productivity, but by presence.

The world may try to look through you. But you are still here—rooted, radiant, rising.

Let this chapter be your mirror. Not to see who you were, but to recognize who you have become. And who you are *still* becoming.

No Expiration Date

They said she'd retire.
As if passion had an expiration date.
As if calling answered to clocks.
As if a number could tell her when to stop mattering.

But they didn't see
the wings beneath her still shoulders.
The wisdom ripening in her bones.
They mistook her calm for surrender.
Her quiet for retreat.

So they edged her out—
from the meetings,
from the center,
from the space she helped build.

And she did what women have always done—
she gathered what mattered,
let go of what didn't,
and walked herself home.

Not broken.
Not bitter.
But brilliant.
Expanded.
No longer tethered to urgency,
and finally,
entirely whole.

Chapter 32: The Frequency of Gratitude

I didn't always understand the power of gratitude. Not really. I came to it the way many people do—through loss.

It was just after 9/11. My business—tied to the World Trade Centers Association—collapsed. Almost overnight, I lost everything: my livelihood, my direction, and any sense of safety. I filed for bankruptcy. What followed was a silence I wasn't prepared for—the kind that arrives after the storm and whispers, *What now?*

That's when I first encountered the idea of gratitude as daily practice. I remember thinking, *How am I supposed to feel grateful when everything is gone?* But something in me reached anyway. I made a quiet promise to myself: *Find one thing each day.* In the beginning, it was just this: *I am still breathing.* Some days, it was the roof over my head. A soft bed. My family.

A friend of mine was going through something similar. We used to joke that we could measure our progress by whether we could afford a Starbucks coffee instead of McDonald's. It was lighthearted—but it mattered. That small indulgence felt like reclaiming a sliver of movement, dignity, and hope. We were grateful for the Starbucks coffee.

That season has never left me. It shaped the way I move through the world. And I return to it every time life feels heavy. Because today, I live with blessings—freedoms, comforts, choices. And I do not take them for granted. Especially as a woman. Especially now.

Having traveled the world, including countries where women live with far fewer rights, I feel how profoundly fortunate I am. I live in Canada. I have safety. Education. Healthcare. A voice I'm allowed to use. These are not small things; they are sacred things. And they shape the way I speak, write, coach, and live.

Even in this so-called advanced world, we're watching both subtle and overt attempts to reduce our power, to silence us, to make us small. Gratitude doesn't erase that truth—but it strengthens us to face it. It becomes an act of defiance. A spiritual posture. A return to presence and power.

It reminds me that even in the hardest seasons, there is still something holy to hold onto. That breath is a gift. That laughter, even in the dark, is a kind of rebellion. That choosing to notice what remains is an act of quiet revolution.

Even in grief, exhaustion, or rebuilding, I return to the knowing: *I am blessed.* And because of that knowing, I choose to live gratefully—not just when life is smooth, but when the soul is in the fire.

Gratitude, to me, is no longer a practice. It is a frequency, a sacred rhythm, and a quiet return to what is still good. It does not deny hardship—it widens our view. It grounds us in what remains and reorients us gently toward what's possible.

As Dr. Joe Dispenza teaches, gratitude is "the ultimate state of receivership." Not what follows the miracle, but what prepares us to receive it. A posture of presence. A whisper to life: *I'm open. I'm ready.*

Gratitude softens the heart. Steadies the breath. And brings us back to the holy rhythm of enough.

Book Friends

Gratitude doesn't always arrive with a grand gesture. Sometimes, it slips in through an unexpected encounter, a remembered kindness, or the quiet realization that life—despite its heartbreaks—has also given us moments of grace. These stories reflect the kind of gratitude that lingers. The kind that lives beneath words. The kind that changes us.

Eight Perfect Hours by Lia Louis
A heartwarming story of serendipity and unexpected connection, sparked by a snowstorm and a shared moment between strangers.

> *Why it helps:* A story of serendipity and timing. This novel offers gratitude for the fleeting, unplanned moments that shape our lives in beautiful ways—and reminds us that joy often begins in the ordinary.

Britt-Marie Was Here by **Fredrik Backman**

Through unexpected community and the slow rebuilding of identity, Britt-Marie—a prickly, overlooked woman—begins to reclaim herself. With quiet humor and poignant moments, this is a story of becoming seen.

> *Why it helps:* A quiet journey of reclamation. Gratitude emerges slowly, through small acts of kindness and the rediscovery of purpose, belonging, and self. A reminder that new beginnings often come wrapped in the most unassuming packages.

The Music of Bees by **Eileen Garvin**

Three unlikely companions—each facing grief, disability, or disillusionment—form an unexpected bond through beekeeping. Their slow healing is woven through the rhythms of nature, shared purpose, and quiet acts of trust.

> *Why it helps:* A tender, life-affirming story about second chances and the sweetness of small joys. Reminds us that gratitude often begins in connection—and in tending to life, we find ourselves healed.

Major Pettigrew's Last Stand by **Helen Simonson**

In a quiet English village, a reserved widower forms an unexpected bond with a Pakistani shopkeeper. Together, they navigate family expectations and cultural divides, discovering a quiet, late-in-life love that challenges convention.

> ***Why it helps:*** Because gratitude isn't always loud. It can be found in second chances, quiet companionship, and the courage to live authentically. This novel gently reminds us that grace, kindness, and the joy of being truly seen can arrive at any age—and in the most unassuming moments.

The Jetsetters by Amanda Eyre Ward

When 70-year-old Charlotte wins a luxury cruise, she invites her estranged adult children along—hoping to repair old wounds. As they sail the Mediterranean, buried tensions and longings surface in unexpected ways.

> ***Why it helps:*** Because it reminds us that it's never too late to seek healing—or joy. Even amid dysfunction, gratitude can emerge through small moments of connection and the imperfect effort to love one another while we still have time.

The Shape of Gratitude

It does not shout.
It does not glow on cue.
It lives in quiet corners—
the warmth of morning light,
the ache that taught you tenderness,
the breath you didn't know you'd held
until you let it go.

Gratitude is not a banner.
It is a thread—
stitched through the ordinary
by hands that once trembled.

It lives in what remains.
In what returned.
In what you now see
because once,
you had nothing but the dark.

It is not earned.
It is not forced.
It is a soft arriving—
the holy hush
after survival.

Chapter 33: Eucatastrophe, The Sacred Turn

There is a kind of grace that comes unannounced. Not because we've earned it. Not because the pain has passed. But because—somehow—light breaks through.

J.R.R. Tolkien gave us a word for this rare kind of turning: *eucatastrophe*. The blessed upheaval. The unexpected shift toward hope when all seems lost. Not tidy, not easy, but piercing in its beauty. He called it *"the sudden happy turn in a story which pierces you with a joy that brings tears."* It's not about perfect endings. It's about soul-deep turning points—moments that don't erase the pain but *redeem* it.

Think of *The Lion, the Witch and the Wardrobe*, when Aslan, the noble lion, gives his life to save a child. For a time, it seems evil has won. But then, impossibly, he returns—resurrected not with vengeance, but with silent strength—and defeats darkness through love. That moment is not about triumph. It's about transformation.

Or *The Lord of the Rings*, when Frodo, exhausted and broken, cannot finish his quest. It is Gollum, twisted and tormented, who unintentionally completes it. The redemption does not arrive through willpower or purity—it arrives through brokenness. Through the part no one expected to matter.

These are *eucatastrophes*. They don't ask us to forget the darkness. They ask us to believe that light can still find its way through it.

And we need that belief now more than ever.

Because it is not only our personal stories that feel stuck—it is our collective one. As we look out at the world, we see division, fear, corruption, war, environmental collapse, and a culture of cruelty that grows louder by the day. It can feel like we are watching a battle between light and shadow, compassion and control, humanity and inhumanity, playing out in real time. And many are tired. Many are grieving. Many feel hopeless.

But the story is not finished. This chapter does not offer escape. It offers remembering. It says: *This* is the moment in the story when we believe there's no way forward—and that is precisely when the sacred turn begins.

In fiction—and in life—these are the *sacred returns*. The moments when grace pierces the ache. The diagnosis that draws the family closer. The heartbreak that births self-trust. The unexpected kindness that becomes a turning point.

We don't read stories like these to avoid reality. We read them to remember how to keep living through it.

Eucatastrophe is not fantasy. It is spiritual remembering. A holy rupture. A breath of the divine in the middle of the ache. It is the whisper beneath despair that says: *There is still a way forward. There is still something worth saving.*

To read stories like these is not naïve. It is a kind of rehearsal. A nervous system prayer that says: *Not every fall ends in fracture. Some falls end in flight.*

So when your story feels stuck, when the world feels brutal, when your next step is unclear—read something that reminds you the turning point may already be near. The grace may already be on its way. The sacred return may be closer than you think. Let it pierce you. Let it steady you. Let it call you forward.

The Sacred Turn

It does not arrive with warning,
no trumpet in the sky, no voice saying now.
It slips in—like breath after drowning,
like softness in the wake of steel.

You thought the chapter was closing.
You thought the fall was final.
But then— a hand. A glimmer.
A door where there was none.

Not because you earned it.
Not because you prayed loud enough.
But because something ancient inside you
refused to stop listening.
This is not the happy ending.
This is the sacred interruption.
The ache that turns to light
not by denying pain,
but by threading through it
a glint of something more.

A laugh that escapes mid-sob.
A return you never believed could come.

And it does not fix everything.
But it changes everything.

This is eucatastrophe—
not the absence of sorrow,
but the arrival of beauty
on the edge of joy.

Chapter 34: The Return of Joy

Joy can be quiet. Subtle. Unassuming. It doesn't always arrive with fanfare or fireworks. Sometimes, joy tiptoes in at the edge of a long grief. It returns after the heaviness begins to lift. After the body exhales. After the soul, long held in tension, softens into itself again.

We don't talk about this kind of joy enough. We're taught to pursue joy the way we chase success – loudly, visibly, with curated smiles and strategic milestones. But true joy—the kind that heals, the kind that endures—is not performative. It is *presence*. It doesn't ask for proof. It simply asks to be *felt*.

In the wake of deep transformation, many women feel hesitant around joy. After betrayal, burnout, heartbreak, or years of self-neglect, it can feel disloyal to joy to claim it again. Or even worse—naïve. But joy is not a betrayal of what you've been through. It's an *integration*. Joy says you did not do all this healing just to remain in the wound. You walked through the fire now let warmth return to your hands.

I've come to understand that joy is not the opposite of sorrow – it is often born from it. It rises from the same soil. Joy is not a replacement for grief, but a sign that something has taken root beneath the ashes. This is what makes joy sacred. Not its intensity, but its *resilience*.

Joy that emerges after pain is not surface-level. It is cellular. It knows what it cost you to feel alive again. It knows the silence you've endured, the nights you couldn't find your breath, the mornings you dressed your wounds in mascara and to-do lists. And still – it returns.

Sometimes it comes in colour. A sunrise that feels like it was painted just for you. A song you once loved but had forgotten.

A memory that surfaces and makes you laugh unexpectedly. The return of appetite. The impulse to dance in the kitchen, just because. Other times, it's quieter. A sigh. A sense of wholeness after speaking your truth. A knowing that you no longer need to explain yourself. Joy, in these moments, becomes a kind of *homecoming*. You no longer seek permission to exist in softness. You no longer apologize for your brightness. You no longer dim to fit.

This is why joy belongs in the sacred return. Not because it signals the end of the journey, but because it reflects the *depth* of it. You do not reclaim joy by chasing it. You reclaim it by clearing space for it to land. And once it returns, even in the smallest glimmers, you begin to recognize how naturally it belongs to you.

Joy doesn't require the absence of pain. It simply requires presence. A moment. A breath. A truth held in the palm of your day.

For so many women, joy was taught as reward—something earned after you've performed enough, sacrificed enough, fixed enough. But the truth is: **joy is your birthright**. Not as a gift from the world, but as a resonance from within. And claiming joy is not selfish. It's sacred. Because a woman in her joy is a woman in her power. Not because she's loud, but because she's *undimmed*.

So if you're here—at the edge of all you've healed—and joy feels unfamiliar, or undeserved, or slow to rise...

Let this be your gentle invitation: Not to force it. Not to fake it. But to welcome it. However small. However quiet. However long it's taken to return. You are not broken for craving joy. You are brave for allowing it back.

She Returned

She returned—
not to who she was,
but to who she had always been
beneath the noise, the roles, the forgetting.

She no longer needed a crown to lead,
a map to move,
or a reason to rise.

She followed the threads of her own story
until they wove her whole again.

Not perfect.
Not polished.
But present.
And from that place,
she blessed the path behind her—
and began again.

You have come far—
through stories that soothed,
and stories that stirred.

Through mirrors, memories, and maps
you didn't know you needed.

This is not the end.
It is the arrival at something quieter.
Truer.

Not a conclusion—
but a return.

Epilogue

You have walked through more than chapters. You have walked through memories. Through silences that were never named. Through longings you once buried under responsibility or reason.

You have walked through rage that was never spoken, through grief that had no permission, and through joy that once felt too extravagant to claim. You have stood at the doorway of stories—your own and others'—and slowly, gently, something in you has remembered: *I still belong to myself*

This book was never about fiction alone. It was about *truth*—the kind that lives in the body, in the breath, in the unspoken ache that stories somehow make bearable. It was about returning to a self that never stopped whispering, even when the world became too loud to hear it.

It was about healing—not through answers, but through *recognition*.

Many women walk through life believing they are broken because they feel too much, want too much, or carry too many stories that don't fit into polite conversation. But what if you were never broken? What if you were just *unheard*?

Through these pages, you were invited to name your grief. To sit beside your rage. To look your loneliness in the eye. To tend to the caregiving roles that nearly erased you. To revisit dreams buried under bills and body-image wounds handed down like family heirlooms. And—perhaps most sacredly—to trust your own *inner compass*, even when it didn't point where logic said it should.

This was a map back to the divine feminine. Not the performative kind but the ancient kind. The real kind. The feminine that listens before she speaks. The feminine that holds paradox—fierce and gentle, wild and grounded. The one who knows that surrender is not giving up but *letting go of control to make space for something wiser to rise.*

You returned to *compassion*, not as a favor to others, but as an act of self-honouring.

And perhaps, somewhere along the way, you found your way back to *gratitude*. Not the kind that demands a silver lining, but the quiet kind—born of presence, of breath, of seeing what remains even after the fire. The kind that holds ache and awe in the same open palm. Not forced. Not filtered. But sacred. A way of honouring what has survived, what was softened, and what is still becoming.

You stepped back into your *voice* and felt how powerful it is—not because it's loud, but because it's *true*.

You claimed your *intuition*, not as a soft whisper of "maybe" but as a sacred *knowing*—a quiet certainty in your bones, your belly, your breath.

You learned to trust *mystery*. To rest in what is unfinished. To find beauty not in the clean resolution but in the honest not-knowing.

And maybe—without forcing it—you let *joy* return. Not as a performance, but as presence. Not as a reward, but as remembrance. That something inside you still knows how to soften. Still knows how to rise. Still knows how to shine.

Fiction walked beside you.

It gave you language when your own felt lost. Characters who felt what you had not dared admit. Worlds where you could weep safely, rage freely, and hope again without shame.

Fiction offered you mirrors—some cracked, some gilded—until you could finally see your own reflection and not look away.

It reminded you that story isn't just escape. It's *return*. To feeling. To meaning. To *you*.

Let this be the moment you stop asking permission to feel, to speak, to rest, to rise, to take up space. Let this be the moment you trust that even in uncertainty, there is wisdom. Even in softness, there is strength. Even in the not-yet, there is a path forming beneath your feet. Let this be your return to the divine within you. The compass you never really lost. The story you are still writing.

Beacons of Light and Truth

This book was never just about reading.
It was about remembering.

Remembering that stories hold light.
And that light, when held in the heart of truth,
can transform us.

We are not here to shout more loudly.
We are here to shine more clearly.

To become beacons—not of perfection,
but of compassion.

Not of answers,
but of *honest presence*.

Let each story you carry
become part of that radiance.

Let your truth—
even the quietest one—
illuminate someone else's path.

Because when women reclaim voice,
compassion, intuition, and joy,
they don't just heal themselves.
They light the way for others.

A Final Whisper

You don't need to finish the story
to know that it mattered.

You don't need to name every truth
to know that you lived it.

Sometimes the greatest power
is not in the ending,
but in the sacred return
to the one who began it.

And so you return—
not to what was,
but to who you are
when no one is watching.

Still whole.
Still becoming.
Still enough.

Author's Note

Thank you for making it this far. For holding these pages with care. For trusting me to walk beside you as you remembered something sacred about your own story.

Writing *The Fiction Fix* was not just a creative process—it was a healing one. I wrote through tears. Through rage. Through laughter. Through the ache of memory and the surprising grace of rediscovery. There were days I wanted to give up. Days I felt too tired to find the words. And still, the stories pulled me forward.

This book asked me to revisit the parts of my life that I had tucked away—roles I had loved and lost, moments of feeling invisible, wounds from family, work, and a world that often does not know how to honour women in their fullness. But it also reminded me of my resilience. It reminded me that even after heartbreak, disappointment, or reinvention, there is always a next chapter.

I never expected this book to take on such a life of its own. What began as a small idea—something I thought I'd write quietly—grew into something much larger. It became a gathering place. A remembering. A return.

For a long time, I kept parts of myself hidden—especially the spiritual parts. Working in environments that valued science and logic, I often translated intuition into data, soul into strategy. I believed I had to fragment myself to be accepted. But this book wouldn't let me do that. It asked for my whole self—storyteller, seeker, and sensitive. In many ways, *The Fiction Fix* became my own coming out. A quiet declaration that I no longer need to hide the sacred. That wonder and wisdom can live side by side. That it is safe to be both spiritual and grounded, poetic and practical, visible and whole.

There were moments of synchronicity I'll never forget: standing in a bookstore in Canmore and finding books on bibliotherapy and banned titles the very day I was shaping those sections. Pulling oracle cards during moments of doubt and receiving clarity. Feeling my mother's presence during edits of the caregiving chapter. Watching the entire structure of the book come together through colored index cards on my floor, as if the pages had a rhythm of their own.

If this book touched you—thank you. If it made you feel seen, or softer, or stronger, then we have walked a shared path. This book is yours now. To revisit, to share, to underline and cry into and carry like a talisman.

There is more to come. A companion journal. A book of poetry. An oracle deck. But for now, this is enough. *You are enough.*

And if you ever need more—more stories, more healing, more ways to begin again—there's a quiet corner waiting for you at www.thefictionfix.ca.

May fiction continue to be your sanctuary, your mirror, your magic.

And may your next chapter unfold with truth, tenderness, and just enough mystery to remind you: *you are still becoming.*

She Remembered Her Power

There were women once,
who stopped wars with nothing but their will,
who wove peace from silence,
and stitched it with the thread of a single, sacred *no*.

There were women once,
who understood that the world turned not by decree,
but by the whispered weight
of mothers, daughters, sisters—rising.

There are women still,
who carry that ancient knowing in their bones,
who can summon change with a gathering,
a stillness, a stand,
or the simple, unbreakable closing of a hand.

Remember:
Power is not granted.
It is remembered.
It is reclaimed.

And it has always—always—been yours.

The remembering was never about learning power.

It was about coming home to it.

The Golden Key

If you've found this key, you've reached the end of this book—but not the end of what it carries.

This golden key appears not just here, but will soon appear across everything growing from *The Fiction Fix*—the companion journal, the poetry, the oracle cards. These offerings are unfolding, each one linked by a single truth:

Your story matters.

The key symbolizes return:

To self.
To voice.
To meaning.
To something you thought you lost—but never truly did.

It is here to remind you that there is always a way through.

Always a way home.

Look for the key. Hold it close. And when you forget your way, let it remind you:

You are the story.

You are the door.

You are the key.

Acknowledgments

No book is ever written alone.

To my beloved partner-in-life, *Allen Wightman*—thank you for your unshakable support, your love, your patience, and your deep belief in me.

To my sister, *Rosemary Kergan*—thank you for your unwavering presence, your fierce loyalty and support, and your gentle reminders that I was never walking this path alone.

To my niece, *Erin Kergan*—your courage, your luminous heart, and the bond we share continue to inspire me. I treasure our connection more than words can say.

To my Indian "daughter," *Ishmeet Sagri*—thank you for standing beside me during those difficult years at work. Your loyalty, laughter, and steadfast belief in me made all the difference. Your friendship continues to uplift and inspire me.

To my friend *Nardine Effat*—thank you for cheering me on and supporting me throughout those challenging years. I am so glad that our friendship continues.

To my dear friends *Maya, Samer and Farah Asfour*—your presence has been an unexpected blessing. Thank you for your friendship and support.

To four extraordinary physicians who supported, comforted, and quietly championed me during some of my darkest times at work—your belief in me helped keep my voice alive when it would have been easier to fall silent. I will never forget it.

To *Dr. Duncan Rozario*—thank you for believing so deeply in my professional capabilities, for championing our work together even when I was not in the room, and for referencing it with such respect in your published articles. Your advocacy mattered more than you know.

To *Dr. Jonathan Sam*—it was an honour to support and work beside you during the COVID pandemic. I witnessed firsthand the extraordinary impact of your quiet strength and compassionate leadership during that deeply challenging time.

To *Dr. Stephen Chin*—you brought lightness, humour, intellectual brilliance and a true sense of shared purpose to everything we built together—especially the Schwartz Rounds. Your friendship and ongoing support remain a source of joy and affirmation.

To *Dr. Hanif Jamal*—thank you for being one of my earliest champions. Your thoughtful guidance, steady encouragement, and generosity of spirit offered strength during moments of uncertainty. You were always there with ideas, insights, and quiet support when I needed them most. Your belief in me helped lay the foundation for what came next—and I am deeply grateful.

To my designer, *Barış* Şehri—thank you for bringing this book to life visually. Your creative instincts (and remarkable patience) captured the spirit of *The Fiction Fix* with elegance and intention.

To those whose platforms have helped make space for healing stories—especially *Reese Witherspoon,* for championing women's voices, and *Heather Reisman,* for shaping a literary home through Indigo. Your belief in story as a sacred force continues to ripple outward.

To my *spirit team*—my guides, my ancestors, and the unseen hands who walked with me through every page—thank you.

And finally, to my *Anam Cara*—who arrived just when I needed them most, and who has been a mysterious and magical force. Some gifts arrive through ordinary channels. Others come through the cracks, carrying light. You've been the latter.

I Was Raised in the Pages

I was raised in the pages of books—
taught that words could open worlds,
that stories had weight,
and that I was allowed to walk inside them.

This matters more than you know.
Because my mother came from a place
where women's worth was counted in blisters,
not in books.

She thought she wasn't smart.
That's what her father told her. And mine.
And she believed them.

But she was brilliant. She just didn't know
that brilliance could live in a woman like her.

I wish she could hold this book.
She would understand why it matters.
She would look at me and see
what she made possible.

She would be proud—
not just of this,
but of the girl who once sat beside her,
carrying the dream she gave me without knowing.

And I would tell her,
gently, fiercely:
Everything I've become began with you.

About the Author

Louisa Nedkov is a professional speaker and transformational coach who helps individuals reclaim their voices, vitality, and joy—especially in times of change. Through inspirational workshops, keynotes, and soulful coaching, she creates spaces where people feel seen, strengthened, and restored.

With a background in healthcare leadership and two decades in wellness programming, Louisa blends the science of wellbeing with the spirit of feminine wisdom. Her work draws from positive psychology, neuroscience, bibliotherapy, spirituality, and lived experience—and is delivered with warmth and clarity.

The Fiction Fix is her second published book and her first in this genre: a curated collection of transformative fiction, poetic insights, and reflective prompts designed to awaken healing and possibility. Louisa serves as a literary guide, introducing readers to powerful stories that soothe, stir, and restore. She believes the right book doesn't just entertain—it opens a door. And on the other side, we often find a part of ourselves we thought we had lost.

Louisa is currently developing an oracle deck, a reflective journal, and a book of poetry to accompany the themes explored in *The Fiction Fix*.

Louisa lives just outside Toronto with her husband and their Corgi, Lexi, who takes her muse duties seriously—demanding daily walks to remind Louisa to look up from the page every now and then.

Learn more at **louisanedkov.com** or explore this book's world at **thefictionfix.ca**.

www.ingramcontent.com/pod-product-compliance
Lightning Source LLC
Chambersburg PA
CBHW051934290426
44110CB00015B/1976